MULTIMEDIA TOOLS FOR MANAGERS

MULTIMEDIA TOOLS FOR MANAGERS

Bohdan Szuprowicz

HF
5718
.S983
1997
West

amacom

American Management Association

New York • Atlanta • Boston • Chicago • Kansas City • San Francisco • Washington, D.C.
Brussels • Mexico City • Tokyo • Toronto

This publication is designed to provide accurate and authoritative
information in regard to the subject matter covered. It is sold with the
understanding that the publisher is not engaged in rendering legal,
accounting, or other professional service. If legal advice or other expert
assistance is required, the services of a competent professional person
should be sought.

Library of Congress Cataloging-in-Publication Data

Szuprowicz, Bohdan O., 1931–
        Multimedia tools for managers / Bohdan Szuprowicz.
                p.   cm.
        Includes index.
        ISBN 0-8144-0254-2
        1. Business communication—Technological innovations.
    2. Interactive multimedia.   3. Multimedia systems in business
    presentations.   4. Management—Communication systems.   5. Management
    information systems.   I. Title.
    HF5718.S983   1997
    658'.00285'66—dc20   96-9492
                                                                          CIP

Printing number

10   9   8   7   6   5   4   3   2   1

Contents

Preface: Productive Management With Multimedia

Interactive multimedia communications is one of today's most strategic and effective management tools for enhancing productivity and competitiveness. Strategically implemented, multimedia ensures the survival and growth of competitive business enterprises. Organizations that ignore the multimedia communications revolution will find themselves losing market share and slipping behind lean, downsized competitors and brash new ventures.

Multimedia communications transmission of information among corporate workers is more productive and efficient than through traditional means. It combines voice, text, data, graphics, animation, images, and moving videos into a simultaneous stream of coordinated information, enabling the user to make decisions, solve problems, and acquire necessary knowledge. Properly designed, multimedia communications equips managers with better tools to transmit policy, train employees, and present new products and services to customers.

Interactivity enhances multimedia communications by providing a means for rapidly focusing on pertinent information or knowledge. Realtime interactive multimedia conferencing collaborative sessions unite experts, technicians, business analysts, financial sources, and administrators into efficient decision-making work groups. Collaborative multimedia applications provide data and images transmission and transmit immediate reactions of the participants.

Interactive enterprises that can design and implement effective realtime multimedia communications at all corporate levels have the advantage over competitors that continue to rely on conventional project management. Large or small, these enterprises are tomorrow's virtual corporations, capable of providing customized products or services to any client, anywhere in the world, at any time, faster and more effectively than ever before. This new organizational form comes into being for the purpose of exploiting new business opportunity and disappears after the market is exploited or becomes unprofitable.

Today is the time to think about and plan tomorrow's interactive multimedia communications—even with existing network infrastructures that may not have the capabilities to handle massive data traffic. Hardware, software, and telecommunications vendors, aware of market deficiencies, are racing to develop new products and services to make realtime interactive multimedia communications an effective and cost-effective reality. Managers jumping on the information superhighway can expect a fast, and sometimes bumpy, ride to new global markets and business opportunities.

Development of faster and more powerful processors, massive multimedia storage systems, and interactive multiuser technologies are creating infrastructure elements at an accelerating rate. This development is enhanced by the potential of massive consumer markets promoted by the combined resources of the telecommunications, cable TV, broadcasting, publishing, and movie industries.

An increasing number of companies are taking advantage of interactive global networks and hanging electronic shingles on the Internet. However, the Internet, a prototype for interactive multimedia communications through its World Wide Web, has an insecure infrastructure and is too unpredictable to be a competitive business management tool. Nonetheless, it is important to explore Internet's potential without falling into the trap of seeing it as an existing solution automatically providing a competitive advantage.

This book is a quick-start manual for readers who need to understand interactive multimedia communications and its significance to their organization's future. It discusses major concepts, explains technology basics, and provides the background for knowledgeable decision making and negotiations with technicians and vendors of systems and services.

It takes into account the need to upgrade existing information systems infrastructures. Many organizations already have significant investments in hardware, software, and employee skills, which they must protect. Certainly many existing infrastructures can be upgraded and converted into effective multimedia communications tools.

Another aspect is the need to acquire new, specialized skills—not only to develop effective multimedia communications systems but to participate in new virtual corporate marketing schemes and opportunities. Just-in-time training offers unique opportunities not previously available.

The process of creating multimedia content and applications requires special insight and understanding. There are special issues of creativity, content sources, permissions, image quality, and target audiences that must be addressed at an early date in order to ensure timely completion and avoid legal action and production delays.

The largest part of this book consists of descriptions and evaluations of actual multimedia implementations in corporate business environments. The most strategic implementations are discussed in detail, and readers are provided with examples of successful applications and proven methodologies and resources. They can glean from these descriptions the necessary implementation steps.

The book also contains detailed presentations of profitable concepts and applications: conferencing, training, sales and marketing, presentations, work group computing, and multimedia networking.

Terminology is explained in a comprehensive glossary of concepts, systems, products, standards, hardware, software, content creation, quality control, data compression, transmission, and international standards.

Finally, the book has an appendix listing hardware, software, communications, and service vendors offering specific products and services for design and development of multimedia communications systems. It contains vendor names, addresses, and telephone and fax numbers.

After reading this book, you'll be able to participate knowledgeably in discussions of the alternative technologies, business solutions, required skills, and resources for developing a realistic budget to implement interactive multimedia projects.

1

Interactive Multimedia Communications

Any organization that can interact with its marketplace faster and more effectively than its competitors will quickly become a leader in any of its market. Indeed, interactivity is the underlying concept of the most competitive weapons of modern enterprises. It is not a new concept, for it already exists in all corporate environments at various levels and between various groups of workers, managers, clients, and suppliers. In most cases the interactive operations are isolated, using a single medium of exchange, for example, voice, memorandums, documents, images, or video presentations. All such activities represent communications between various parties that are designed to further the business of the enterprise. When the whole world operates along similar lines, this is all well and good, but these isolated communications are not the most efficient way to transmit all the necessary information. Information technology offers better and more effective means of communication, and limited use of them leads to loss of competitiveness and perhaps loss of market share or even liquidation.

Information technology is used to automate many of the interactive functions within a company and theoretically boosts productivity. But it also produces massive amounts of information, huge databases, and knowledge repositories. What often results is information overload, which is straining human capabilities to interact effectively with the data and with each other.

Interactive multimedia offers a better way to communicate by using the latest information technology advances to advantage. The basic concept is to provide rapid and simultaneous access to all pertinent sources of data and information using the most effective media. When extended to all parties involved, interactive multimedia communications becomes a new management tool that is the foundation for the competitive interactive enterprise.

Defining Multimedia

The simplest definition of **multimedia** as a concept is as follows: the integration of text, data, graphics, animation, audio, and video elements *into a single application.* Such an application may be either a completely passive presentation, comparable to television programming, or a highly interactive realtime networked system requiring multiple end users to make decisions, choose alternatives, take tests, receive advice and training, and purchase goods and services.

The basic premise of interactive multimedia is rooted in the fact that (1) real life is a continual changing experience and (2) information systems that consist primarily of static text and data displays do not mesh very well with daily human activities. Animation, audio, and video introduce the element of motion into information systems, making them more interesting, challenging, and absorbing.

Integrating all the media elements into a smooth presentation is a considerable challenge. While text, data, and many graphic inputs can be entered into a computer system quite readily through a keyboard, or copied from a diskette where they already exist in digital format, this is not so with other forms of multimedia data types. These include documents, animation sequences, voice, audio sounds, music, video, or film. You need special devices—microphones, scanners, video cameras, and audio and video boards—to capture such inputs and convert the signals into digital format for storage and manipulation in a computer.

Once all of the elements are available in digital format you still need special software to edit and integrate the elements into a continuous and synchronized multimedia presentation or application. Then the applications can be deployed on standalone or networked PCs and workstations that are specially equipped so that they become multimedia platforms. Exhibit 1-1 illustrates the various media elements and their relationship to a multimedia application.

Digitization and manipulation of various media elements requires massive amounts of storage and fast processors be-

Exhibit 1-1. Basic multimedia concepts.

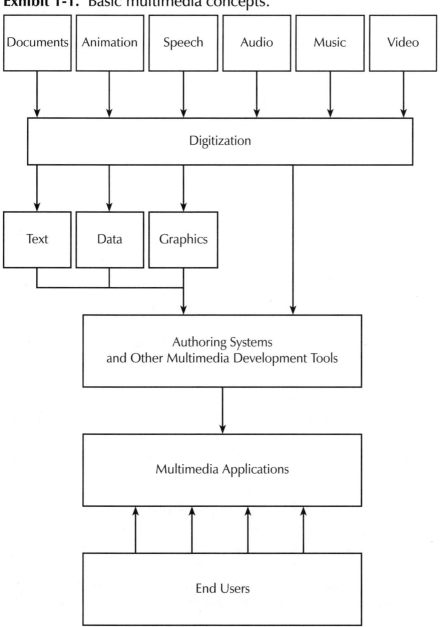

cause the volumes of digitized multimedia data are several magnitudes larger than those for conventional text and numbers processing. Hardware and software **compression** (encoding data to take up less space), special audio and video and accelerator boards, and CD-ROM disk drives are major devices that handle these problems and make multimedia computing a reality. Some conventional computers can be upgraded to multimedia development or delivery platforms through special conversion kits, but the trend among competing vendors is to develop new PCs and even notebooks with built-in multimedia capabilities.

Perhaps the most important fact to keep in mind about interactive multimedia communications is that the various technologies that make it possible already exist. Those are not always the most cost-effective, but their prices are coming down rapidly, and early users in all types of industries are embracing these technologies. Moreover, organizations that are reengineering and downsizing are looking to interactive multimedia communications as a way to provide necessary information to work groups.

The Benefits of Interactivity

Interactivity is basic to passive multimedia information systems because it engages the attention of end users. Studies have shown that actual involvement and personal experiences make a much greater impact on human beings than passive observation and absorption of sounds and video images. Today, interactivity can range from a simple hypertext retrieval of documents by a single worker to realtime, multipoint multimedia conferencing with simultaneous transmission of files, spreadsheets, images, videos, and sounds.

Interactive systems can be equipped with **smart agents** and intelligence to assist corporate workers and managers in making decisions. Additionally, they can be equipped with checks and balances to prevent managers from making incorrect or disadvantageous decisions and to monitor the performance of all enterprise workers at all times. When deficits in knowledge or skills are discovered, the interactive multimedia system is the perfect vehicle for providing **just-in-time training** and advice to all workers within a group.

Interactivity Is All Over the Enterprise

The everyday operations of all enterprises are a conglomerate of a multitude of interactions at various levels. In order to understand the potential of interactive multimedia communications, it pays to look in some detail at the interactivity that already exists in a typical organization.

Most corporate environments already contain many examples of interactive systems, but they are seen as separate activities, unconnected with each other and often incompatible. In some cases, interactivity operations require network transmission facilities with sufficient **bandwidth**—that is, transmission capacity—to satisfy specific end-user expectations. In others, the interactive operations are strictly stand-alone applications, using only a basic PC platform and a **hypertext software program** (where interactivity is limited to the digital text or document only).

You must also understand that there are great differences in interactivity requirements. End users interested primarily in local information or knowledge retrieval do not need the same system capabilities as those involved in realtime multipoint conferencing with users widely scattered throughout the world. The requirements of the different networking segments interconnecting such islands of interactivity within and outside an enterprise will vary greatly, and they therefore present a complex integration problem if they are to operate smoothly and seamlessly. The good news is that the technologies for linking all such interactive operations into a realtime multimedia communications system exist. Of course, organizations that want to introduce these systems will have to reassess the way they have done business. Companies that choose to do this, and sooner rather than later, will gain a significant advantage over their competitors.

Categories of Interactivity

As shown in Exhibit 1-2, interactivity is broadly classified into three categories of transactions: user to document, user to system, and user to other users. Within each category are different levels of user involvement, depending on access interfaces, distribution and broadcasting facilities, and manipulation of multimedia elements. The levels of interactivity increase from completely passive user roles to predominantly active operations, where the user must constantly take the initiative to participate in the interactive activity.

User to Document

The simplest example of interactivity between users and documents is hypertext and **hypermedia applications**—products that allow the user to retrieve and manipulate certain graphic, image, and video elements. Most hypertext and hypermedia files are based on CD-ROMs for use with stand-alone multimedia platforms, although specialized corporate hypermedia applications may be based on interactive systems that allow updating to take place. At the distribution and broadcasting level, corporate videos are prepared for information purposes and distributed through networks to desktop users or specific

Exhibit 1-2. Levels of interactivity.

Interactivity	User to Document	User to System	User to Users
Access interfaces	Hypertext, hypermedia	Graphical user interfaces	Conferencing, training
Distribution and broadcasting	Newsletters, memorandums	Internet, information kiosks	Presentations, interactive TV
Objects manipulation	E-mail, videomail	Databases, Æles, archives	Groupware, multipoint videoconferencing

information kiosks strategically deployed throughout the corporate campus. Interactivity here is limited to access by end users at a time most convenient to them, and often information may be downloaded into local storage for future viewing.

Videomail, also known as multimedia-enabled e-mail, also fall under this category. Here the user can access messages in specific locations, as well as create messages for transmission to others in predetermined locations. The most important characteristic of this type of interactivity is that the user is severely restricted in the ability to influence and manipulate the contents of these files.

User to System

The more sophisticated operations category of end user to system interactivity is characterized at its basic level by **graphical user interfaces** (GUIs) that provide the user with numerous choices of action through selection of representative icons. **Authoring systems,** which allow the development of tutorials, and Windows-based applications are excellent examples of this genre of software. They allow interactive access to a wide variety of tools that can be used for development of multimedia applications plus many other computer applications, multimedia or not. This type of interactivity is not time sensitive, although it may provide access to software tools that can be used to develop and store multimedia applications.

User-to-system interactivity is well represented at the distribution and broadcasting levels by public networks like the Internet World Wide Web (WWW) or private kiosk-based multimedia applications. These range from relatively simple information dispensers to sophisticated merchandising systems with considerable built-in intelligence and transactional order-taking capabilities—for example, a bank-owned kiosk in a shopping mall that offers a wide array of services to users, from ordering checks to verifying account balances. Interactive multimedia kiosks are designed around a specialized server and use local or wide area networks (LANs and WANs, respectively) for distribution and updating of content. Corporate closed-circuit video distribution networks are also representative of this category. The important fact to remember here is that the end user is basically the receiver of information from such systems.

At the highest level of user-to-system interactivity are the multimedia databases, multimedia data managers and files, and object-oriented databases capable of handling multimedia data. Many of these systems represent multimedia storage facilities. Users must be skilled at operating the various authoring systems and editing programs. The important concept at this level is that the user can manipulate the system contents by changing their characteristics (color, size, texture, or shape). Using a combination of software tools accessible by way of the GUIs, users can design original multimedia objects and capture existing images, sounds, or videos for storage and later manipulation. Interactivity in and out of such systems is growing in importance with the development of collaborative multimedia systems and service.

User to User

Interactivity between users (or among many users) is clearly the area that will contribute the most effective interactive multimedia communications tools and systems for the future. It operates in realtime to create responses between two or more users. Multimedia applications in this category are time-sensitive events and demand the highest bandwidth and processing speeds on networks and transmission facilities. Many of the communications in this category are sensitive to transmission delays and irregularities, so the infrastructures must be designed with great care to provide acceptable results.

Conferences Between Participants

At the lowest level in this category are the various forms of conferences between participants; they often include presentation and inspection of documents, texts, graphics, images, and videos. All forms of corporate training, with one or a few users instructing or teaching much larger groups of workers, fall into this category as well.

Presentations to Large Groups

At the distribution or broadcasting level, such conferences turn into one-way presentations to large groups of people with only very limited means of interaction—for example, questions at specific times. Also falling into this category at this level is the new medium of interactive TV, a means to reach large numbers of consumers through the existing TV networks made interactive through the use of special set-top control units. Interactive TV provides users with numerous choices of what to see when they want to see it. Plans for the future include electronic catalogs and home shopping.

Interactive multimedia presentations are another use here. A small group of users controls the broadcast of multimedia information to larger audiences. Many conferences now use this technique to illustrate speeches with videos of product operations. The objective is to discover group preferences or establish consensus through realtime feedback and manipulation of the presentation. This type of interactivity requires special presentation facilities, including large screens and audience response units, and it may require the use of wireless communications.

Groupware and Multipoint, Multimedia Networks

Groupware and multipoint, multimedia conferencing networks are the most complex interactive communications systems. These provide direct communications between two or more parties who expect to use such facilities, which are much like conventional telephone networks. Multimedia conferencing systems vary in complexity depending on whether these are point-to-point, person-to-person, multipoint, multiuser, or multiprotocol implementation. They may represent virtual conferencing between parties, or corporate training and just-in-time instructional sessions. Such complex high-capacity networks represent real-time interchanges between parties and require considerable bandwidth capacities and high-performance processing systems.

The most sophisticated form of user-to-user interactivity is multimedia **groupware** (software designed for use in a network that serves a group of users working on a single project) and **telecollaboration** (multimedia conferencing coupled with simultaneous realtime capabilities for manipulating objects, images, drawings, text, and videos among all those participating). Interactivity at this level requires extensive multiuser communications infrastructures with high bandwidth capacity and speedy access to various multimedia databases and storage systems. Concurrent and simultaneous engineering practiced in manufacturing industries are representative of this type of interactivity.

What Collaborative Multimedia Is All About

The collaborative multimedia process is the ultimate interactive multimedia communication. Here, numerous workers are always engaged in conversations with each other from a variety of geographic locations. Whether an interactive multimedia system is justifiable among such groups depends on the level of worker proximity and the frequency of communications.

If the groups are located far apart in distant cities or foreign countries and a lot of telephone and fax traffic, transmission of data and documents, and travel is involved, there are good reasons to consider interactive multimedia communications facilities for telecollaboration. How many collaborating workers will justify a multimedia network of this type is hard to pinpoint because the decision depends on the length and frequency of conversations, volume of information, images, and data exchanged.

Technological Resources

This type of interactive multimedia communications is demanding of networking and data processing resources. It requires several simultaneous transmission channels because each workstation in the network must be able to generate one outgoing channel of multimedia audio and video as well as accept and decode several other channels originating from all the other collaborating stations. Organizations interested in these capabilities face significant investments to upgrade their LAN and WAN systems to handle multiple streams of multimedia data in realtime. Still, managers considering such systems should be aware that interactive multimedia conferencing can be handled successfully as long as there are no more than six to ten other workstations. A number of studies indicate that conversations within groups larger than that become extremely difficult to control and may even be counterproductive.

Early adopters have implemented multimedia conferencing systems with relatively few nodes (connection points). The Advanced Technology Group at Apple Computer, for example, began using twelve nodes in a network, and another corporation uses fifteen nodes. Motorola has a thirty-node system installed in its business communications group, and the multimedia network at Aetna Life links many branches of the company with over one hundred nodes. Other early adopters with multimedia conferencing networks are the federal court system, Ford, Hewlett-Packard, Kaiser, and Levi-Strauss.

User Groups

Managers overseeing the design of an interactive multimedia communications system of this category must differentiate and define the user groups—usually company employees and contractors with different levels of responsibility. As a result, there are issues of access to sensitive data and network security that must be considered from the start. For example, it is important to ensure that intermixing of data and inputs from various sources in realtime does not threaten corporate confidentiality. Consideration must be given as well to users who may want access to multimedia communications environments from time to time but are not actual participants in interactive conversations—for example, top executive observers, trainees, and other workers who need to be informed about interactive events and their results, in either realtime or after the fact and without the participants' being aware of such supervision.

A complicating factor is the existing communications infrastructure, typically one that has grown over the years yet with a mainframe-based information system that remains critical in day-to-day operations. Managers must determine to what extent the infrastructure can be upgraded, and at what cost, to develop a multimedia communications environment to meet the requirement of all conversational communities within an enterprise. If yours is a **virtual corporation**—one that must accommodate the temporary collaborations of unpredictable interactive groupings and enterprises within and outside an organization—you need to build in considerable flexibility. If your organizational reengineering has been extensive or you have formed a whole new entity specifically designed to act as a virtual corporation, your interactive multimedia communications system may have to be designed from the ground up.

When Interactive Multimedia Communications Is Justified

The actual requirements for interactive multimedia communications ultimately depend on the needs of the targeted audiences. A NYNEX study undertaken to support the development work on the Media Broadband Services (MBS) network found that collaboration within an organization is established and maintained primarily by various forms of **conversation.** These interactions between groups and individuals develop into networks of relationships pursuing a common objective and result in collaboration and the accomplishment of work.

Conversation encompassed a number of fundamental concepts that make it useful and must be emulated in an interactive multimedia communications system; among them, expression, articulation, response, exchange, dialogue, and improvisation. These are so important to the interchange that they must not be restricted by inflexible procedures, so typical of traditional computing environments. Rather, they are necessary factors in the design and implementation of a successful interactive multimedia communications environment. Certainly, economic factors will eventually prevail, but keep in mind that a system must reflect actual conversational realities and practice; otherwise, it will be doomed to failure.

Interactive Infrastructures

User Interface

The design of the electronic conversational environment at the user interface is an important factor. Users must be able to manipulate all the multimedia elements—text, data, graphics, animation, audio, and video—so that the interface reflects actual conversational situations as much as possible. In multimedia conferencing, for example, the capability to display images of participants simultaneously in windows on a single screen becomes an important feature. In fact, most desktop conferencing software limits the number of images that can appear on the screen at the same time, although many include the capability to change images in windows at will. A valuable feature automatically indicates or highlights the image of the person who is speaking at that time. These interactive conversational aspects with variable multimedia elements in a system make multiparty videoconferencing attractive and desirable.

The extent to which a system can display multiple images and indications about each participant depends on the number of channels that the network can handle simultaneously, which in turn depends on the overall bandwidth of the network and bandwidth of the individual end-user connection.

Electronic conversational environments offer features that provide insights that are not normally available within conventional conversations. One is that every participating end user can bring his own image into one of the windows on the screen and observe his own behaviors and reactions during interaction with the other participants. In other words, every participant can see how all the other participants perceive him or her during conversations.

System Potential

Interactive multimedia communications systems that can handle multiparty videoconferencing are the latest, and most complex, management tools. Although all of their advantages and disadvantages are not yet fully understood, they clearly have great potential—for example, for providing timely information or training, or for developing consensus. There is a sense that interactive multimedia communications in which all members of a group participate and record their contributions facilitates consensus building and decision making. These systems can also record and store the interactive conversations for future review and analysis. They can capture the nuances of body language and voice intonations of the participants in a way that cannot be done now.

Security Considerations

The possibility of a permanent record of collaborative sessions creates a new environment, one that managers must understand and learn to control. Because these are potentially sensitive areas of corporate activity, decisions must be made early about the various access and security levels that control the storage and transmission of multimedia materials, in realtime or after the fact. Rules and practices must be established to control private two-party or desktop-to-desktop multimedia interactions between top-executive decision makers preceding or following more general consensus-building collaborative sessions.

For the most efficient operations, all systems should be able to integrate seamlessly with each other, but for political reasons, multiple access checks, controls, and monitoring systems must be put in place. Managers must not lose sight of the additional expense that such requirements will impose on the total cost of these systems.

What Kind of Interactive Traffic Will There Be?

Managers must determine in advance to the best of their ability the types of multimedia data that will be transmitted through an interactive multimedia communications system. Installing realtime multiparty videoconferencing capability at every desktop is the ideal situation but probably not cost-effective, at least until high-performance communications links exist throughout the company. Nevertheless, individuals or groups holding conversations should be able to acquire, interpret, manipulate, and transmit various multimedia elements: text, graphics, animation, images, voice, music, film and videos, as well as strictly programming-related objects, such as data, code, and frames of information.

If you are in charge of designing an interactive multimedia communications system, you must determine the types, volumes, and sources of multimedia objects that will be manipulated and integrated in the network. You can then include the appropriate hardware and software tools and will be able to decide on the required bandwidth of various network transmission segments.

There is a bonus to this approach: exposure at an early stage to the issues of ownership of many multimedia elements that will be included in the system. Managers may control multimedia content which may not see the light of day unless sufficient networking capabilities are designed into the system. An example would be visualization videos requiring very extensive storage and high-speed transmission facilities. If the various elements that will be used originate from sources outside the enterprise, permissions and licenses must be obtained so that the items can be incorporated in the system. This question of permissions and licenses extends to the participants in the system, particularly when their statements are recorded for future analysis or possible public use. Multimedia storage requirements can be massive—well above those used for conventional data, as well as specialized multimedia databases, filing systems, client-servers, and video servers. These are new solutions specifically designed for handling multimedia files. You will also have to establish special limits and yardsticks for measuring the importance of multimedia data for storage in order to optimize the operation of the new system.

The Importance of the End-User Interface

The end-user interface should be *very* user friendly, to the point where it can be used without effort by the most computer-illiterate workers. This means an interface with simple and attractive controls that anyone can understand and manipulate.

Initiating an interactive multimedia communications session should be as easy as making a telephone call. The critical aspect here is simplicity, for complex interfaces may put off potential users.

Although interfaces have been developed for specific end-user populations, this approach may be very expensive, particularly when the actual end users of the system cannot be predicted with any certainty. Probably the best solution is a common user interface that is easily understood by the greatest number of potential end users. Another possibility is that vendors are developing interactive multimedia applications for many existing productivity programs—word processors, spreadsheets, database systems, and the like. As a result many GUIs that already exist within various products allow customization of the user interface. Once interactive multimedia communications networks are better established within an organization and costs come down, in-house information technology experts can customize the interfaces with features and facilities that optimize the operations within that organization. Managers must make sure that the customization process does not interfere with or degrade the overall interactivity levels and collaborative objectives and that it lends itself easily to periodic updating.

All of these aspects of interactive multimedia communications must be addressed when these modern tools are being introduced to an enterprise. Keep in mind that your competitors will also be developing their own interactive multimedia communications systems in the drive for efficiency. The competitive advantage will then depend solely on the excellence of the interactive multimedia communications system and its ability to capture and transmit the most profitable market intelligence. This above all must be the guiding principle as you evaluate and then implement interactive multimedia communications.

2

New World Order Competitive Forces at Work

Since the early 1990s, several technical, economic, and social factors have been leading toward the multimedia revolution.

Innovative progress has been made in hardware and software technologies. The GUI is a good example of the direction in which solutions are being sought and an encouraging step on the road toward wide use of interactive multimedia communications. Semiconductor industry advances provide new generations of microprocessors and memory chips at rapidly declining prices. They result in shorter product cycles and more powerful platforms for handling massive volumes of data cost-effectively. Object-oriented programming concepts and high-level authoring systems are the new software vehicles used to develop easy-to-use interactive multimedia systems.

Business factors in the new world order are also at play as enterprises recognize that customer satisfaction and superior product quality are key to their survival. The intensifying global competitive environment demands extensive customization of products and services and continuous training and re-training of workers. Interdisciplinary development teams driven by product quality and the need to be first to market are necessary to meet these challenges. It is quickly becoming impossible to compete effectively without an infrastructure of highly interactive multimedia communications and end-user interfaces. In addition to acquiring, manipulating, and transmitting massive volumes of data and information in the course of doing business, corporate workers are also exposed to a variety of training and orientation programs that increase in frequency as product life cycles get shorter and process complexities continue to increase. The hierarchy of these converging factors is illustrated in Exhibit 2-1.

Exhibit 2-1. Hierarchy of converging multimedia forces.

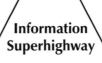

Information Superhighway

Interactive Content

advertising, corporate training,
information services, business
presentations, kiosk merchandising,
value-added networks, entertainment,
health care services, video games

Distribution Services

high-speed telecommunications, cable TV networks,
video-on-demand services, interactive TV,
digital wireless, personal digital assistants,
videoconferencing services, cellular, direct broadcast satellites

Enabling Technologies

fast 32-bit and 64-bit computer platforms, optical storage systems,
data compression technology, object-oriented software, collaborative
computing, multimedia authoring systems, digital signal processing,
fiber optics, video servers, high-speed switching equipment

Political and Economic Pressures

intensifying global competition, shortening product life cycles,
continuous corporate training requirements, information overload,
better customer services, Wall Street investment euphoria,
national and international policy

Information:
The New Unlimited Form of Capital

Information is now considered the new and unlimited form of capital, but this is true only if the information is captured and manipulated rapidly into knowledge, which is then communicated, received, understood, and acted on quickly by the right people. If the knowledge is not presented in ways that facilitate rapid collaborative decision making, it is not useful. Managers without the proper information evaluation and transfer tools are in danger of floundering and even drowning in an ever-increasing flood of data and market research. (Worse, a competitor with a more intelligent system may capture that information.)

How much information can human beings absorb and use effectively without losing perception of its priorities and importance? Information overload is overwhelming large numbers of managers and workers alike, and corporations are looking for answers to this question. Computer screens full of text and numbers are not the best means to deliver information effectively. Nonelectronic information is not the solution either because it cannot be accessed and acted on fast enough.

The introduction of multimedia communications, with both voice and video, can go a long way to alleviate some of these problems. Development of smart agents to perform a lot of analytical tasks automatically is even better. Perhaps most important to keep in mind is that anyone with a workstation and a modem can access huge amounts of information, wherever it may reside in cyberspace, from anywhere in the world. This is the basis for a whole new global competitive environment in which those who move faster and more efficiently than their competitors will survive.

Organizations that supply products and services must reorient their operations and see customer satisfaction as the ultimate business objective. Such an approach means superior product quality, faster design and manufacturing cycles, extensive customization, superior customer service, and continuous training and retraining of increasingly mobile and temporary workforces.

The Global Competitiveness Imperative

The new world order is being perceived as three powerful blocs—North America, the Far East, and the European Community—competing for customers within and outside their territorial borders. Companies that today are operating without global ambitions are at risk of losing their markets to more competitive foreign marketing organizations.

Over time, these three marketing blocs will consolidate their economies and compete vigorously with each other for market share. The European Community, in the formative stages for several decades, is finally entering the phase of full economic integration. The North American Free Trade Association (NAFTA) is combining the economies of the United States, Canada, and Mexico into a more integrated trading bloc, which may expand to Central and South American economies in the future. And Japan continues to be the Far East powerhouse, while collaborating closely with manufacturing bases in South Korea, Hong Kong, Singapore, and Taiwan. These Pacific Rim countries are flooding the world with new products that have often displaced and even destroyed Western industries.

The rest of the world is important too. The emerging market economies of Eastern Europe and the new republics in the formal Soviet Union present huge new markets. Moreover, they are home to large and highly educated scientific and engineering populations eager to undertake complex design and manufacturing tasks at a fraction of the cost in the industrialized countries of the West and even the Far East. There is also the potential for a Muslim bloc, consisting of the Arab countries in the Middle East which control a major percentage of world oil reserves, and some of the new Central Asian countries that were part of the Soviet Union. Some oil-rich states have the financial resources to acquire the latest automation and information technologies. They thus have the potential to create a highly competitive trading bloc and to manipulate the supply and distribution of capital, products, or services anywhere in the world. Exhibit 2-2 illustrates the relationships of these trading blocs.

Exhibit 2-2. Global trading blocs.

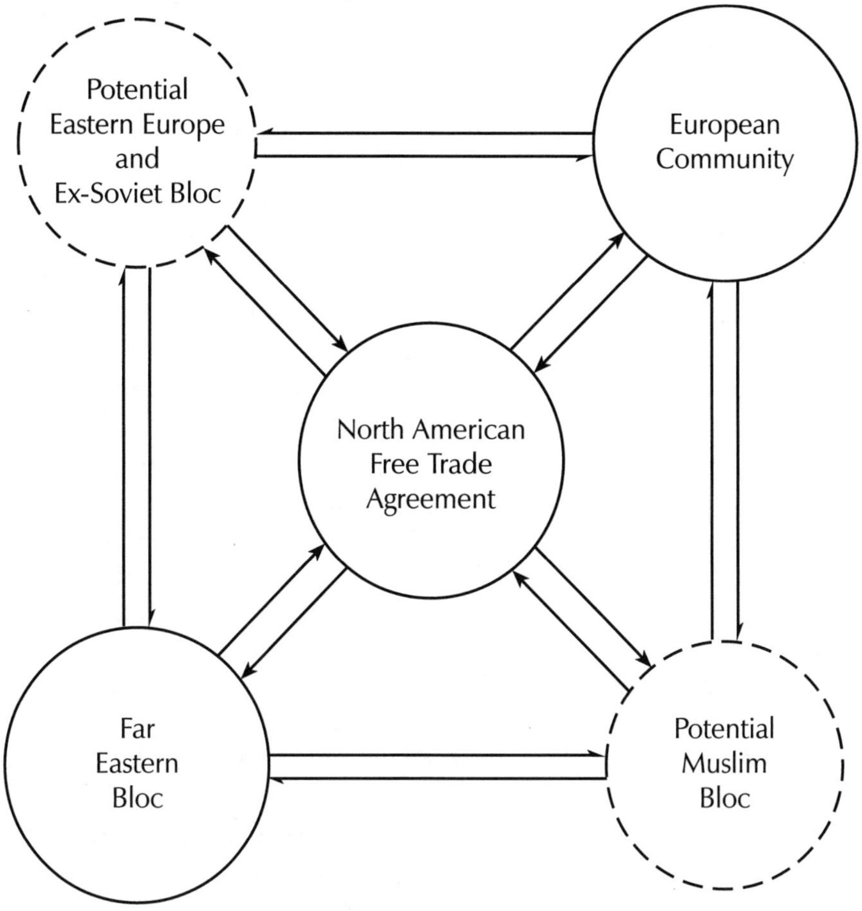

Political and Economic Pressures

Intensifying global competitiveness is probably the major influence driving corporations and countries to become more efficient suppliers of goods and services. One aspect of this
competition is the ability to identify and evaluate quickly the
most efficient development and production facilities for a product for which corporate intelligence discovers a market. Because of global networking services, time is of the essence;
sooner or later all competitors will discover the same business
opportunity. The winning supplier will be the first corporation
that puts together the most cost-effective organization to design, develop, produce, deliver, and service the product.

This type of activity is facilitated with interactive multimedia communications, which also make it possible for suppliers in any part of the world to take advantage of a market once they have assembled all the necessary information and skills. Some governments—Israel, for one—have created national programs for developing interactive multimedia capabilities throughout the country for developing products and services for domestic and export markets. Many more countries will follow suit as they recognize new opportunities for employing their populations and improving their living standards without dependence on geographic location or natural resources.

France's parliament enacted a new law in December 1994 guaranteeing universal access to interactive multimedia communications to all its citizens. The new law also stipulates that high-bandwidth interactive multimedia networks will cover the whole country by the year 2015. A national interactive multimedia network organization is being established to examine priorities for implementing interactive applications for education, training, and business and cultural objectives.

Many other countries will also work to develop global connectivity and networks such as the Internet to their advantage whenever they can. Forrester Research estimated that at the start of 1995 3 million users worldwide were connected to the World Wide Web multimedia servers of the Internet. Projections are that this number will grow to 10 million as early as 1997 and to 22 million by the turn of the century.

A Vision of Massive New Markets

Major cable TV, communications, entertainment, and computer industry companies are trying to position themselves to take advantage of what most experts believe will be massive new markets once digital interactive multimedia technologies are introduced. The vision of 500-channel cable TV networks that are expected to appear during the next few years is a powerful incentive for product and service vendors. They see a rapidly growing demand for specialized microchips, new video servers, massive storage systems, intelligent TV control units, better communication networks, and innovative interactive applications and services and worry about their future if they do not jump on the bandwagon.

The most attractive interactive multimedia business potential will be in the following traditional market segments, whose annual revenues total about $120 billion in the United States alone:

- Catalog shopping
- Broadcast advertising
- Home video
- Information services
- Recordings (records, tapes, and compact discs)
- Movie theaters
- Video games
- Cable advertising
- Electronic messaging
- Videoconferencing

Catalog shopping is by far the largest of these, estimated at $51 billion and perceived to be among the best opportunities for exploiting interactive multimedia technology (see Exhibit 2-3). As a result of these market visions, an emerging multimedia industry is taking shape, encompassing semiconductor manufacturers, computer systems and peripherals, consumer electronics, video-game suppliers, software developers, broadcasting, publishing, advertising media, as well as cable TV, telephone, wireless, and videoconferencing communications services.

The perceived size, potential for rapid growth, and associated publicity of all the multimedia market segments is attracting companies large and small, which want to participate in what appears to them to be a new-media communications era. They include the well-established entertainment and broadcasting empires, as well as entrepreneurial firms that fear losing control of their existing markets, and perhaps even their businesses, if they do not take advantage of new opportunities.

The complexity of interactive multimedia communications in business, industry, and consumer and educational markets is reflected in the range and variety of companies that provide the basic components—hardware, software, and content—and

Exhibit 2-3. Top ten markets for interactive multimedia business potential.

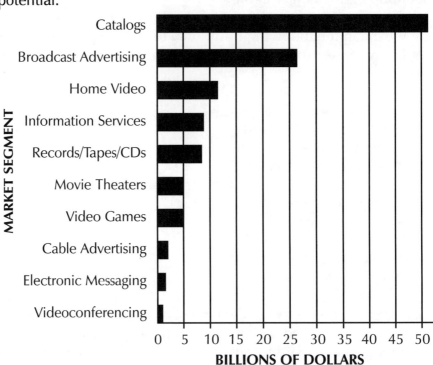

Source: Computer Technology Research Corporation, "Multimedia Networking and Communications."

distribution methods to the various end-user populations. Additionally, new specialized ventures are emerging, offering more efficient multimedia products and services than those of established technology companies and consultants are specializing in the design and implementation of these large and complex projects.

Convergence of Enabling Technologies

Hardware and software products are making multimedia processing easier and cheaper. Of the estimated 200 million PCs installed in the world, about 15 percent are either capable of handling multimedia applications or can be upgraded. Moreover, there has been rapid growth in the delivery of new multimedia-capable computer platforms to the end users in consumer and business markets alike.

According to Dataquest estimates, worldwide shipments of multimedia PCs in 1994 amounted to 10 million units, for a growth rate of 316 percent over the 2.5 million units shipped in 1993. Multimedia PCs, designed to deliver multimedia applications, are basically PC platforms equipped with audio boards, CD-ROMs, and speakers. Because the prices of these multimedia peripherals are declining rapidly, multimedia capabilities increasingly are being built in to new PC products. This upgrading in itself is a powerful incentive to implement interactive multimedia communications since the latest PC platforms do not require additional investments and are not fully utilized unless they run multimedia applications.

In sum, corporate managers more often than not are being handed the hardware tools for implementing interactive multimedia communications in their organizations. How well they will exploit this opportunity depends on their choice of appropriate software tools and applications and the speed with which they can deploy such systems relative to their competitors.

All of these changes are coming about as a result of the accelerating progress of the semiconductor industry. Semiconductor manufacturers are not very visible, but they nevertheless are crucial to the multimedia communications revolution because they supply increasingly more powerful microprocessors that are essential for developing new PC and workstation platforms for handling multimedia data efficiently. Essentially this process more than doubles the capabilities of processors on the market every eighteen months, a rate that is expected to continue well into the next century. Of course, this also means that any hardware on the market is obsolete almost as soon as it is installed.

Digital signal processors (DSPs), which can rapidly translate analog signals of the real world into digital patterns, are considered the crucial technology for making multimedia hardware increasingly practical and cost-effective. DSP sales are growing at over 31 percent annually, and multimedia-related DSPs are by far the fastest-growing segment. These products include basic multimedia DSP chips that can handle realtime operations in partnership with host processors, DSP-based audio and video **codecs** (coders/decoders), dedicated compression chips, and audio DSPs for music and voice applications. Advanced Micro Devices, Analog Devices, AT&T, Hewlett-Packard, IBM, Intel, Motorola, National Semiconductor, and Texas Instruments are all involved in multimedia microchips design and manufacture.

Computer hardware vendors perceive multimedia as an enabling technology that will increase the use of computing platforms, particularly PCs and workstations. They are also aware that their technologies are crucial to the development of interactive multimedia services in the massive consumer market and are setting up alliances with organizations in the telecommunications and entertainment industries. Several have developed special video server hardware and software specifically to facilitate the processing, storage, and transmission of interactive multimedia traffic.

Market research suggests that about 80 percent of all multimedia platforms will be IBM and compatible PCs, including Windows-based PCs and multimedia PC (MPC) platforms. These will predominate in corporate training, presentations, referencing, and personal multimedia delivery. Macintosh multimedia platforms are estimated to account for about 15 percent of the total and are expected to dominate in multimedia production, interactive kiosks, and desktop video publishing. Multimedia conferencing increasingly will dominate multimedia communications, and leading videoconferencing vendors are moving to exploit networked PC platforms in preference to their existing proprietary videoconferencing systems.

Powerful workstations are seen as excellent devices for providing client-servers for LANs, transactional kiosks, multimedia production, and concurrent engineering applications. In addition, peripherals such as CD-ROMs, audio and video boards, scanners, erasable optical disk drives, video cameras, and speakers that enable standard computing hardware to handle multimedia are now widely available.

A Wealth of Multimedia Software Tools

Software in the multimedia industry takes on a special—and broad—meaning, for it includes operating software, multimedia development tools, and content materials (documents, archives, films, images, videos, books, magazines, artwork, and complete libraries of special items). Among the multimedia software tools are authoring systems, animation, audio and video editing, graphics, and multimedia design utilities. Some of these software products are being developed by major hardware manufacturers, but more often, new, specialized multimedia software ventures are teaming up as business partners with major computer firms. Microsoft, the largest software company in the world, has even greater ambitions when it comes to multimedia markets. The company has built-in multimedia networking capabilities in its Windows NT and 95 operating systems.

New multimedia software products and ventures are being created almost every day, with better and easier-to-use products.

Multimedia Networking and Distribution

Telephone and cable TV companies are among the most active players trying to grab a stake in the interactive multimedia communications business. They are rushing to control as big a market share of the digital superhighway of the future as they can. Telephone companies already have access to almost all American households and cable TV exists in 60 percent of homes with higher speed connections. Telephone companies are ahead with digital switching technologies, but most homes are wired with low-speed conventional wires so they are developing compression schemes and expanding high capacity connections to handle multimedia transmissions.

By the year 2000 about 40 million homes are expected to be linked directly by fiber-optic networks, and those who control that access will be well positioned to capitalize on interactive multimedia traffic and services of all types.

Long-term trends in the entertainment industry—primarily TV viewing and movies—indicate a shift from advertiser-supported to consumer-paid viewing, with pay-per-view developing as the major delivery mode. Digital networks are particularly attractive to broadcast organizations under these circumstances because they provide an inexpensive way to replicate entertainment whenever audiences want it. This means faster and larger returns on investment, plus the ability to obtain precise demographics about specific audiences and end users. Interactive TV system developers can pinpoint to advertisers which particular second in a commercial generated a product order or interest.

The mammoth broadcasting and entertainment industry—encompassing ABC, Paramount, Columbia, Time Warner, and others—are naturally attracted to multimedia networks because they control large archives of intellectual properties such as movies, photographs, music, and various types of data banks. Deregulation trends, which allow TV networks and studios to merge and own cable services, are also significant factors in motivating broadcasting organizations into interactive multimedia communications.

Interactive Content Is Available

Publishers of books, magazines, and newspapers and more specialized companies like broadcasting organizations and movie studios all own vast archives of information, images, and various forms of knowledge of value in training, education, and entertainment. Many publishers have already taken the first step into interactive multimedia communications by developing CD-ROM-based versions of encyclopedias and specialized books, where images, sounds, and video sequences enhance such products.

Most CD-ROM titles today are primarily databases—directories, lists, statistics, and the like—and are targeted at the stand-alone PC user with a CD-ROM drive. However, the growing numbers of interactive CD-ROM players that hook up to TV sets suggests that publishers eventually may be able to exploit digital networks to provide direct services to users in the form of electronic magazines, electronic books, and complete multimedia databases of their products. Publishing firms are also interested in distributing CD-ROM-based versions of their titles directly to record and bookstores as distributor channels to include interactive multimedia products in their outlets.

A whole new crop of ventures and boutiques are specializing in the development, storage, and selection of multimedia content materials for the production of interactive multimedia applications. Corporate managers today need not worry about creating a multimedia development team and searching for the various skills that are required. They may do so if the corporate multimedia development effort is going to be sustained and extensive, but there is so much talent already available that it is probably more effective to purchase products and services from outside suppliers. What is needed to make a proper judgment is some knowledge of available interactive multimedia applications and how they can be used to enhance corporate productivity and competitiveness.

These ready-made interactive multimedia products are being developed by advertising agencies, specialized software companies, training specialists, merchandising ventures, video games developers, and health care information specialists.

System Integration Help Is in Place

The design and implementation of interactive multimedia communications systems is a complex and specialized task, requiring skills that are not always readily available within a company. Indeed, the work is often performed by consultants, who analyze their client's corporate environment and suggest the most appropriate interactive multimedia communications solution. Among these consulting companies are American Management Systems, Andersen Consulting, Booz Allen & Hamilton, CAP Gemini Sogeti, CSC, Electronic Data Systems, and the management consulting arms of the Big Six accounting firms.

Growth in specific technologies is often reflected in the types of projects such systems integrators undertake. Most of those organizations are involved in corporate reengineering projects and act as agents of change. They analyze the markets in which a client corporation operates, assess the resources available for competing, both now and in the future, and recommend solutions suited to the enterprise. Systems integrators are a major force in introducing and designing client-server

environments, which create conditions conducive to the introduction of interactive multimedia applications and communications. This process accelerates with the emergence of new
specialized multimedia systems integrators and niche consultants.

The Time to Act Is Now

Some organizations may not be aware that they lack the skills
and background necessary to implement the most effective interactive multimedia communications systems. Some may not
even believe that interactive multimedia communications is a
topic that they should be concerned about. In these cases, it is
the business managers who must investigate these new management tools and determine their value to the enterprise. Part
of this task is comparing their corporate environment to those
that have already adopted interactive multimedia communications systems.

The technologies, hardware, software, and development
skills are all in place. The knowledge and content providers are
rapidly flooding the markets with multimedia applications,
and service organizations are developing means of transmission and delivery throughout the world. There is no time to lose
in introducing interactive multimedia communications into an
enterprise. Organizations that do not act soon will be dismayed
when their competitors, perhaps even in a different country or
continent, spot the opportunity to enter a market with more
competitive products or services and use interactive multimedia communications to gain an advantage.

International business competition has always been an un-
forgiving activity, and with the spread of interactive multimedia communications, competition is bound to heat up.
Managers who seek to survive will do well to equip themselves
and their organizations with the most reliable interactive multimedia communications tools—and soon.

3

The Virtual Corporation in Cyberspace

Massive workforce reductions and major shifts in the American economy have contributed to changes in the traditional corporate structure. New paradigms have emerged, and employees who stay are empowered with new responsibilities. New interactive enterprises are combining skills and resources to form temporary virtual corporations that exploit market opportunities quickly and more efficiently. Realtime, multipoint, multimedia communications, within and outside the interactive enterprise, provide the infrastructure to make such operations possible.

As more powerful computing platforms become available—at the desktop and in the field linked through a conglomerate of LANs and WANs—businesses will develop into interactive working environments offering new efficiencies and competitive advantages. Multimedia applications, at the core of new solutions, are the realtime interactive infrastructures that provide facilities to make the virtual corporate model a reality. This new corporate paradigm eliminates barriers of time and distance by creating more effective collaboration among participating individuals and entities.

Enterprises need interactive multimedia communications systems if they are to keep in step with the new cybermarkets resulting from extensive PC use and the availability of digital connectivity over public and private networks. Competing with and complementing the PCs in cyberspace are the ubiquitous interactive TV sets wired through cable and fiber links.

Brave New Cyberworld

In the year 2000 about 70 percent of households in developed countries will have some form of computing equipment and half will be linked to online service networks (META Group information technology assessment). Corporate PC users will be communicating with other employees through high-capacity LAN segments in the range of 100 to 150 megabits per second (Mbps). Such workforces will connect with each other nationally and globally through **asynchronous transfer mode** (ATM) backbone, which handles data and realtime video, and WAN networks that automatically provide the required bandwidth on demand.

By the turn of the century, PCs will be running at speeds that are considerably faster than they are today. Miniature magnetic disks will provide the capacity for storing ten hours of video or the text of 20,000 books. Such processing power will be more than adequate to make the desktop or portable PC a videoconferencing terminal with built-in video camera, microphone, speakers, and networking interfaces for universal connectivity.

PCs and infrastructures for interactive multimedia communications are developing rapidly. Worldwide dial-phone services provide direct access to the Internet, voice, video, videofax, and imaging communications around the world.

To be effective, corporate restructuring must take all this into account and plan accordingly.

We have moved into the interactive multimedia age—the third age of computing that is bringing together the computer, the telephone, and the TV into a massive (if chaotic) network within which everything interacts with everything else. Cyberspace can be fun for consumers but hell if you are a business manager who must continually restructure to meet emerging needs.

You must also keep track of changing user populations operating in cyberspace. Aside from networking PC users with enterprises, many online services offer subscribers everything from simple news and e-mail to virtual multiuser conferences. In 1995, subscribers were estimated at 20 million. The number is expected to reach 55 million in 1998. In addition there are an estimated 40 million connected to the Internet expected to increase to 100 million by 1999. What is significant is the rapid growth of PC users linking into the global information super-highway.

Unfolding cybermarkets are too vast, and changing too rapidly, to keep track of without the use of artificial intelligence. You must give serious thought to incorporating into your interactive multimedia communications smart agents—complex expert system routines instructed to wander off into electronic markets or cyberspace in search of prospects, goods, or requested information.

New Ways of Doing New Business

We have already touched on the factors driving the development, introduction, and use of interactive multimedia communications:

- Acceleration of speed and capacity in hardware
- Convergence of computing, telecommunications, broadcasting, and publishing into a global information super-highway
- Continual restructuring of traditional corporate models into interactive enterprises competing globally for market shares of changing markets

Evolving business environments require immediate responses with specialized and competitive resources. Paramount now is (1) the identification of business opportunities through superior intelligence and (2) the rapid creation of knowledgeable teams or groups to take advantage of market opportunities first, before anyone else does.

Upgrading for Better Competitiveness

Competitive corporations realize that advances in information technology are providing new opportunities for growth, but changes in management structure and decision processes are required. Changes can result in faster decision-making processes, better customer services, higher-quality products, as well as increased group productivity and creativity. Corporate multimedia is the infrastructure that can facilitate the envisioned transformation.

Often the applications with the greatest payoff are those that are critical to the delivery of products and services. These implementations usually involve management information systems (MIS) departments and system integration teams that must ensure the needed local and wide area networks to handle the massive, time-sensitive, and unpredictable data transmissions.

Technology alone—no matter how advanced—is not enough to make corporate multimedia successful. Much depends on the content of applications and the presentation. Consider the corporate functions that can benefit from multimedia technology:

Corporate Function	*Multimedia Application*
Communications	Corporate broadcasting
	Executive information systems
	Multimedia conferencing
	Employee information systems
Marketing	Design of commercials
	Interactive advertising
	Product information kiosks
	Promotional presentations
	Customer services
	Virtual reality simulations
Sales	Merchandising kiosks
	Product catalogs
	Buyers' workstations
	Portable multimedia presentations
	Selling advisers
	Personal digital assistants
Training	Corporate training
	Sales training

	Just-in-time training
	Distant training
Product development	Concurrent engineering
	Reference systems
	Simulations
	Product visualizations
	Design advisers
Manufacturing	Diagnostics
	Equipment maintenance
	Testing procedures
Administration	Multimedia file sharing
	Multimedia databases
	Document imaging
	Productivity systems

The Interactive Enterprise Idea

Enterprises today already depend on a number of computing and communication devices and systems, ranging from notebooks and electronic organizers in the field, through PCs and workstations on interconnected networks, all the way to minicomputers and mainframes throughout the city, nation, or even world. To operate effectively, all systems must be able to exchange everything, from simple data files to high-resolution graphics, including multimedia presentations that may include realtime interactive multiparty communications. The essential requirement for universal connectivity—among new and unfamiliar enterprises, customers, and other supporting or regulatory organizations—creates enormous challenges to business entities. Exhibit 3-1 illustrates the interconnectivity.

Individual enterprises that seek to participate in the virtual corporation must have interactive multimedia computing and communications infrastructures that provide for collaborative multimedia computing at the work group, corporate, and inter-company levels on a global basis. Collaborative multimedia in all its forms is a powerful means of internal communications and the technological basis for the market-driven virtual corpo-

Exhibit 3-1. Interactive enterprise concept.

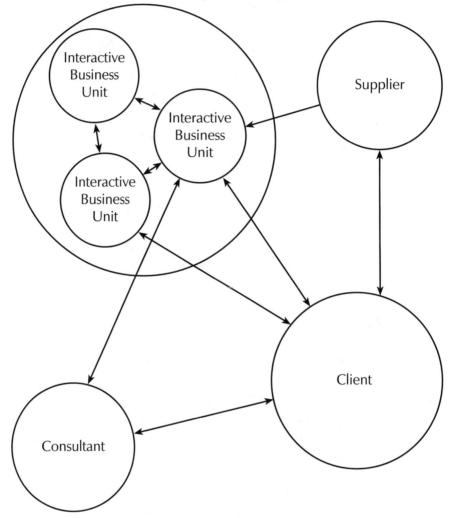

ration. Three technological and organizational requirements are critical:

1. A flexible communications center connecting individuals to the enterprise.
2. Office productivity tools integrated on the desktops.
3. Full transmission capabilities.

This means high-performance workstations (or servers), fast high-bandwidth networking, multitasking, and cross-platform standards with access from remote locations and mobile units.

The Virtual Corporation Objective

Recall the definition of a virtual corporation: a temporary network of independent companies—designers, manufacturers, customers, and competitors—linked by information technology in order to share skills, costs, and access to each other's markets. Pharmaceutical companies with their networks of suppliers, distributors, and medical consultants throughout the world are already well on their way to becoming virtual corporations. Other product assembly organizations in automotive and appliance industries are also nearly there.

This is a highly flexible organism consisting of a group of collaborative units pooling resources to exploit a specific and timely market opportunity. As soon as the opportunity is capitalized on, the virtual corporation typically ceases to exist. (Contrast this concept with the joint ventures, formed on an ongoing relationship to exploit market opportunities not defined clearly at the outset.) Virtual corporations, sometimes known as *modular corporations,* result from seizing market opportunities and are often limited to a single product in a context of fast-changing events. These markets are characterized by rapid growth rates and relatively short product life cycles. Thus, marketing speed and time are critical.

Traditional vertically integrated, self-sufficient businesses cannot respond fast enough to contemporary marketing challenges. The virtual corporation model, however, permits concentration on specific core activities and takes advantage of outside sources (with special skills, patents, or competencies) to develop or manufacture other aspects of the product. This is particularly true of technology-oriented companies—automotive, electronics, and pharmaceuticals, for example.

The virtual corporation implies a competitive advantage and represents the ability to develop and deliver a virtual product or service any time, any place, faster than ever before. It also means a drastic change in mind-set, from mass production to mass customization.

The model relies extensively on information technology, particularly in the interaction between executives and employees and integrated databases containing the timely information and knowledge regarding markets, customers' needs, technologies, products, designs, manufacturing suppliers, and competitors. Companies refusing to reorganize face decline and eventual extinction.

If business reorganization continues at its current rate of growth, the United States will be the leading virtual economy in the world by the year 2015.

Collaborative Multimedia: Interactive Tools of Tomorrow

Interactive enterprises provide facilities for the collaboration of corporate employees with others, anywhere in the world, regardless of time, computer platform, or application. They require extensive use of networks that can handle massive interactive multimedia communications without distortion or delay. Also, there must be multimedia data-handling capabilities and realtime video transmission capabilities of all the interconnecting networks. Often islands of automation must be redesigned to become interactive collaborative networks. The immediate problem is financing the investment in the information technology infrastructure and determining how much of it can be protected until there is an acceptable return on investment.

Virtual Conferencing

The introduction of multimedia elements, particularly realtime audio and video transmissions, makes it possible to conceive of virtual conferencing rooms (or environments) that bring all participants—internally from marketing, research and development, plus outside vendors, distributors, and customers—together at a convenient time. All of these participants can collaborate on a project without leaving their own work-stations, no matter where in the world they are located. The most effective conferences consist of no more than six partici-pants, and most conferencing systems are designed accord-ingly. Nevertheless, several virtual conferences may be taking place simultaneously within an enterprise, and they may be in-volved in multiple projects. Clearly multimedia transmission facilities must have the capacity to handle multiple simultane-ous multimedia transmissions.

As a business manager, you must at least generally under-stand the requirements and limitations of collaborative multi-media systems so that you can choose between high-speed transmission services and construction or upgrading the net-works you already have to carry your anticipated traffic. If your proposed solutions do not take account of all the complexities, you will find yourself reengineering and reinvesting in net-working infrastructures within a short time.

Personal Multimedia: Empowering the Individual

Personal multimedia systems deliver information at any time and in any way an individual wants to look at it. It is a one-way communications tool providing employee training, sales materials, customer service, and some just-in-time diagnostics and factory floor support. Most personal multimedia facilities consist of stand-alone PCs or workstations with multimedia de-livery capabilities in form of a CD-ROM drive and associated hardware and software for handling full-motion video. An in-creasing number of systems are being connected to area net-works, but personal usage is primarily for conventional information processing. Some multimedia platforms provide access to other files that can hold the data. More often, multime-dia products are distributed by way of CD-ROM or laser disks on which interactive applications have been recorded. Very few networks provide for the realtime transmissions required for multimedia conferencing and communications.

The Power of the PC Eruption

An increasing number of PCs are already network connected, and as collaborative computing benefits advance, the number of PCs on networks will increase, a situation that will rapidly create data transmission overload and bottlenecks on the networks. New and faster communication links offering greater transmission capacity will be needed. IBM estimates show 20 million PCs are connected to networks. If at least 15 percent of those are multimedia-capable platforms, this means that several million PCs can transmit and manipulate multimedia data. The percentage may actually be higher considering the number of high-end PCs and workstations equipped with built-in multimedia capabilities.

As a flurry of new products facilitates multimedia or desktop conferencing, an infrastructure will be created that is conducive to the establishment of interactive multimedia communications on a wider scale. Collaborative multimedia computing is the technological basis for the interactive enterprise and the virtual corporation.

Group Multimedia: New and Exciting
Ways of Team Management

Personal multimedia systems provide new ways to deliver information and training to individual workers; the group multimedia network is the first step in developing collaborative multimedia work environments. Group multimedia translates to realtime interactive facilities for sharing screens, whiteboards, images, and other data files in a teleconferencing environment. It provides new ways for project teams to work together. To meet the emerging needs, groupware applications and products are being developed so that each team member can be equipped with a networked PC or workstation with multiple-way communications between team members. The theoretical basis of group multimedia systems is that interaction among project team members with different skills and viewpoints contributes to a more innovative atmosphere and results in better products or solutions.

Typical group activities may include collaborative business analysis and decision making, concurrent or simultaneous engineering, and desktop telephony encompassing e-mail, faxes, voice mail, and specialized interfaces. Group systems also provide an interactive communications infrastructure for financial service organizations with employees in geographically dispersed branches who must work together to review and analyze documents, reports, and database records.

Concurrent Engineering: Product Design of the Future

Concurrent, or simultaneous, engineering is being implemented in firms that design and test new products and machinery. This effort focuses on a specific product or process and combines the elements of desktop conferencing and multimedia file sharing. Concurrent engineering, the generation of engineering process automation following design and drafting and computer-assisted design and manufacturing (CAD and CAM) systems, came into being before collaborative computing was introduced simply because the powerful, networked workstations capable of supporting it were available to engineers first.

The use of these systems generates massive data that must be stored and transmitted to other groups. To reduce error and processing time, the files must be integrated into a common database. More advanced CAD and CAM systems, three-dimensional modelers, rendering and visualization programs, and interaction between such functions cannot be accomplished without collaborative computing systems. As a result, concurrent engineering received early support from companies such as Boeing, British Aerospace, GM, Mazda, NCR, Renault, and Sony, as well as government agencies and leading engineering universities.

Concurrent engineering provides faster time to market, improves quality and performance, and reduces cost. It gives each group in the engineering process an opportunity for immediate discussion and feedback. During the initial design stage of a product, changes and modifications are relatively easy; therefore, early visualization of an end product by all parties (sales and marketing, the client, financing, designers, test engineers, manufacturing and maintenance specialists) can minimize costly changes at a later date.

Because of the heavy use of graphics and visualization, concurrent engineering contributed to the early development of multimedia technologies. Object databases (ODBs)—those that hold abstract data types—were first developed as common files with multimedia capabilities in order to accommodate engineering design objects and information that could not be handled by conventional database products. Concurrent engineering also focuses on the problems of transmitting multimedia objects across networks because most engineering workstations must collaborate with various platforms and differing versions of operating systems and interfaces.

Enterprise Multimedia

If personal multimedia is a new way of delivering information and group multimedia is a new way of working together, **enterprise multimedia** is a new way of doing business. It is the ultimate corporate collaborative multimedia concept, focusing on developing more effective interaction among groups. It seeks better ways to develop products and services and provides new opportunities for improving operations. Information technologies require changes in management structures and decision processes; enterprise multimedia provides the infrastructure that facilitates the transformation. It supplies employee groups with competitive-edge information through better communications. The results are faster decision making, better customer relations, higher-quality products, and increased group productivity and creativity.

Because the entire company is involved, applications with the greatest payoff are those critical to the delivery of products and services. These strategic multimedia implementations usually involve MIS departments and system integration teams that must ensure that all networks can handle the massive, time-sensitive, and unpredictable multimedia data transmissions.

Enterprise multimedia benefits are not realized without the appropriate hardware, software, and networking infrastructure, but it is the applications' contents and presentation forms that play the most vital roles.

Key point: Technology alone cannot make corporate multimedia a successful alternative.

The Information Superhighway: Flashing Lights and Signals

The major telecommunications firms, cable TV companies, and entertainment organizations have entered the multimedia market, with visions of 92 million American households equipped with televisions and telephones and 25 million of them with personal computers. In order to inject interactive multimedia services into this vast market, a digital highway infrastructure is currently underway as a national fiber-optic network.

The Internet plays a major role in interactive communications. It currently connects approximately 21,000 networks in ninety countries and links about 7 million computers used by over 40 million users worldwide. Corporations use it as a cheap, fast, and effective way to exchange information with business associates, customers, and suppliers. Many find it essential to doing business. Many regard the Internet as *the* information superhighway, and for most e-mail and text applications, it is adequate. It is not enough, though, for time-sensitive multimedia transmissions (videoconferencing or realtime groupware collaboration). In order to develop this capability, the Internet must be able to command transmission capabilities on demand and allocate it on a varying basis. It requires additional hardware and software equipment to perform dynamic realtime allocation among multimedia applications, such as videomail, file transfer, and videoconferencing.

If the Internet is to be used for multimedia transmission, it requires a provider with enough transmission capability at all user locations. Internet access providers, however, lease or sell physical connections and hardware, and not all have the greater capabilities.

There are other problems too. Enterprising hackers have violated networks, making security a problem; the introduction of multilayered security schemes has not proved to be the answer. Also, many corporate employees find the Internet difficult to use, and the introduction of newly developed directory services (with added interfaces and referral schemes) to facilitate navigation only creates new barriers.

The World Wide Web, the multimedia aspect of the Internet, provides access to graphics and video materials, though retrieval is unpredictable. WWW will undoubtedly improve, and it is a significant resource to be considered for the overall corporate interactive multimedia communications program. It should not be considered a ready-built alternative for an effective and competitive interactive multimedia communications system, however. Nevertheless, the Web technologies are being increasingly used on internal corporate networks, also known as "intranets."

Interactive Multimedia Communications: Dovetailing Objectives and Applications

The function of networked multimedia applications is to make information technology central to business problem solving. The best example of this is multimedia conferencing, which provides an all-purpose communications facility and is sometimes considered the key of the future.

Networked multimedia applications fall into categories depending on the specific corporate function supported: corporate communications, marketing, sales, training, product development, manufacturing, and administration. Many applications exist to support such functions on a stand-alone basis because networking facilities are not always adequate to handle multimedia traffic and because there were few products until recently facilitating multimedia communications on corporate networks. This situation is changing and many existing applications are prime candidates for upgrading to networked solutions.

> Wise move: Make an audit right away of all the multimedia applications in operation and then evaluate the possibilities of linking with existing networks that offer complementary advantages.

Smart Agents to the Rescue

Many multimedia implementations are similar to **expert systems,** particularly in diagnostics, customer support, help desks, and training. (Expert systems are artificial intelligence systems that solve problems based on data obtained from humans.) Expert systems, originally developed with only text and rudimentary graphics in their knowledge bases, are now capable of handling graphics, images, animation, and audio and video sequences. Multimedia applications, however, are often developed to have particularly user-friendly tools.

In some networked applications, both expert systems and authoring systems are used to develop an intelligent interactive multimedia system. Whether this sort of application is justified depends on the amount of intelligence required to be embedded in a particular application.

Within an interactive enterprise, numerous expert systems will reside in readiness to provide guidance and advice to those who are required to make quick decisions regarding new and unfamiliar issues. Extending this, interactive multimedia communications, in the form of smart agents, search information superhighways for potential clients, customers, products, services, skills, financing, or any other goods and services available in cyberspace. Smart agents also make network intelligence capable of fixing its own problems. They help people find information or services without knowing where these may exist. The advent of smart networks will be a force in the race to be first.

4

Getting Comfortable With the Technology

This chapter talks in lay terms about the basic hardware, software, and peripherals you might need to develop and deploy multimedia applications. It covers the basics, describing in detail the digitization, storage, and manipulation of audio, video, animation, and graphics. It also identifies the methods and tools used to integrate and develop multimedia applications. (Computer literates may find the chapter elementary and skip to the next one.)

Because of the many possible solutions, there are no hard-and-fast rules in developing multimedia applications. It is important, however, to have an understanding of the basic components. You will not need all of the elements covered in this chapter to produce a multimedia application. The ultimate selection depends on your audiences, the hardware and software you already have, your budget, and time deadlines.

Digital Audio: What It Is and How It Works

Some of the simplest applications—annotated e-mail, for example—integrate only text or graphics and sound. For this to happen, the audio component must be converted through an analogy-to-digital (A/D) converter into digital sound that can be manipulated and integrated with other data in a computer.

The most common method for storing and manipulating voice digitally is known as **digital sampling:** The analog-sound waveform is converted to a number at a fixed sampling rate. In order to reproduce a digital sound as close to its original as possible, the sampling rate must be at least twice the highest reproduced frequency. Since humans cannot hear frequencies higher than 20,000 cycles per second (20 KHz), the sampling rate must be at least 40 KHz for best results. The coding to represent sound requires at least 14 bits per sample for full fidelity. That's why 16 bits is the more common number used for top-quality audio sampling. The higher the sampling rate, the better it represents real-world sounds in digital format but requires more storage space and bandwidth for data transmission.

Standard sampling rates are 11.025 KHz, 22.05 KHz, and 44.1 KHz using either 8- or 16-bit resolutions. This means that 1 hour of sound using the top sampling rate requires 44,100 $\times$ 60 $\times$ 60 = 158.74 million samples, equivalent to 317 megabytes (MB) of disk storage at 16-bit per sample for a single channel. Stereo sound requires double that amount. There is a trade-off between sound quality and sampling rates. That's why some multimedia audio components use only 8-bit 22.05 KHz sampling.

Sound digitization may appear simpler than video digitization, but it's not. There is no audio equivalent of a still image, so audio must remain a continuous signal and cannot be treated as a series of individual structures. Audio transmission becomes critical in networked applications where delays in interfaces, such as routers or gateways, can distort the sound beyond an acceptable level. Audio is a realtime operation and must receive priority in a computer when mixed with other multimedia elements. It is referred to as **time-sensitive traffic.** Various techniques have been developed to reduce the data rate. Because audio signals are one-dimensional and do not have a structure, there is no opportunity to use redundancy, as in two-dimensional video,* to achieve compression. Perceptual coders are also used to make up for the human inability to detect certain sound degradations to achieve additional compression. Audio compression ratio is seldom better than four-to-one, based on standard sampling rates, and produces data rates

---

*Similar video frames can be compressed much more effectively because they all contain a lot of redundant data.

of approximately 128 kilobytes per second (KBps) audio channel. Continuing efforts are under way to achieve better compression ratios.

Digitization and compression functions are implemented using special microchips on audio boards that are add-on products introducing sounds into basic PCs. Audio boards are available from most computer sources and can be bought to upgrade existing desktop computers. Major suppliers are Creative Labs, Media Vision, and Turtle Beach Systems. Many PCs today are preconfigured with such boards.

Digital Video: Putting on a Class Act

The most dynamic and desirable element in multimedia applications is **motion video**—a series of still images displayed in sequence at about 30 frames per second (fps) to create the illusion of movement. Some applications use live video images, which include realtime transmissions from TV stations, satellites, video cameras, or VHS recorders of analog video displayed in a window on a computer screen. The images in these displays cannot be manipulated within the multimedia application itself.

Digital video requires conversion from analog signals originating from outside sources into digital format for manipulation and display within a multimedia data stream. All video quality is measured against broadcast TV, which operates with full color on a full-screen basis at 30 fps. In order to provide digital video of comparable quality on a typical 640 × 480 display, it would be necessary to transmit 307,200 pixels 30 times per second, which is equivalent to about 9.2 megabits per second (Mbps). Moreover, to reproduce full color, 24 bits are required per pixel, which brings the total requirements to over 221 Mbps or about 27.5 megabytes per second (MBps), well beyond the capabilities of average PCs and workstations.

Yet although digital video is more demanding on computer resources than digital audio is, perception is more tolerant of video irregularities. In other words, the eye will not notice that a frame or two was eliminated during display, so it is possible to obtain much higher compression ratios with video ranging up to 200-to-1.

Multimedia video presents a number of trade-off possibilities, including the size of the window display, the frame rate, and the color depth per pixel. The minimum frame rate that maintains some perception of motion is about 15 fps. That's why videophones providing no more than 10 fps video result in jerky and uneven motions. The actual video parameters chosen will depend on the actual application, but considerable data storage reductions can be obtained by using a small window of 160 × 120 resolution, with no more than 15 fps and only 8-bit color depth. The 8-bit per pixel color depth is not sufficient to represent true color in many natural scenes; the 24-bit color depth provides up to 16 million colors but requires three times more volume.

To get around the massive data volumes involved, digital video is compressed using hardware, software, or special operating systems features. These tasks are accomplished through the use of video boards, which often include audio capabilities as well. These boards specify their capabilities in terms of image size, basic frame rates, and video requirements, but image quality varies depending on sources and methods employed. And in the final analysis, video quality is judged subjectively by individual users.

About 100 video-board products are available and range widely in price and capabilities. Among the vendors are AITech, Cardinal Technologies, Creative Labs, Digital Vision, IBM, Intel, Matrox, Media Vision, New Media Graphics, Optibase, Radius, Raster Ops, Sigma Designs, Truevision, Videologic, and Xing Technology.

Compression Techniques

Compression and decompression can save storage and display all media elements without affecting sound or appearance in four categories: audio, still images, motion-video, and voluminous text and numbers. All compression schemes are based on some form of redundancy. (The standards discussed in the following sections are summarized in Exhibit 4-1.)

Audio Compression

Audio compression is accomplished by eliminating redundancies between stereo channels and reducing the number of bits in sampling. There is usually little difference between successive samples in an audio channel, and even music mostly consists of frequencies under 4 KHz. This means that 11.025 KHz sampling rates at 8 bits is more than adequate, and compression ratios of two-to-one to ten-to-one are possible.

Exhibit 4-1. Major video and audio compression standards.

Compression Standard	Description of Major Parameters
Joint Photographic Experts Group (JPEG)	Still-image compression standard Photorealistic image quality Obtains ratios up to 200:1
Moving Pictures Experts Group (MPEG) MPEG-1	Major video compression standard Handles up to 1.2 Mbps data streams 352 × 240 resolution at 30 frames per second Provides compression up to 200:1
MPEG-2	A superset of MPEG-1 for broadcast industry requirements Data rates up to 8 Mbps 720 × 480 resolution at 30 frames per second Provides typical compression ratio of 30:1
International Telecommunications Union± Telecommunications Standards Section, Standard H.261	International standard for videoconferencing Enables interoperability between equipment of different vendors Provides 9.115 to 35.45 Mbps data rates

Still Images and Motion Video

The Joint Photographic Experts Group (JPEG) developed a compression standard for still images to transmit gray-scale and color images with photorealistic quality using 24-bit color depth. It compresses images according to variations in color and brightness. Because it loses some color information on decompression, it is known as **lossy compression.** JPEG compression ratios of up to 200-to-1 are possible, and the technique can be implemented in hardware or software.

Video data can either be compressed in realtime as they are being captured and digitized, or after being stored in the system. Video compression exploits the fact that the human eye is less sensitive to color and shade variations than it is to brightness of an image. Compression schemes depend on devising mathematical algorithms that smooth out within digitized video streams all the details not processed by the human eye.

There are two established standards for video, drawn up by the Moving Pictures Experts Group (MPEG). **MPEG-1** is the standard for digital video compression for use with interactive multimedia applications, and **MPEG-2** is designed for broadcast TV and video on demand. The standards are based on intraframe and interframe motion estimation techniques. The algorithm analyzes data in key frames known as **I frames** or intrapictures, and compression is achieved by recording changes from frame to frame. MPEG-2 can support broadcast-quality video and handles data rates up to 15 Mbps, which includes the typical LAN bandwidths deployed in many corporate networks. The best compression results are obtained with MPEG hardware implementations, but MPEG software for video playback also exists.

The **H.261 standard,** drawn up by the International Telecommunications Union–Telecommunications Standards Section, pertains specifically to worldwide videoconferencing communications and attempts to facilitate interoperability between incompatible systems. Until its announcement in 1990, videoconferencing vendors used proprietary codecs that were incompatible with each other. This standard, also known as the px64 standard, outlines the process that all codecs must follow in compressing digital video for transmission.

Text and Numbers

CD-ROMs are optical disks that provide convenient and relatively low-cost storage and delivery for large databases. CD-ROM drives are the basic components for multimedia delivery platforms due to their high capacity (540 MB per disk). Compared with magnetic hard disk drives, CD-ROMs are less useful because they are hard to update directly and are relatively slow. Typical hard drives now average less than 20 milliseconds (ms) in access time, while the best CD-ROMs are about ten times slower, near 200 ms. Magnetic disks also offer faster transfer rates, while CD-ROMs are slower.

CD-ROM drives have become standard computer equipment because of their capacity to store digital sound and video. The latest multimedia PC standards (MPC-2) call for CD-ROM drives with double-speed (300 Kbps) **CD-ROM/Xas,** which incorporate digital audio playback capabilities. Many vendors include CD-ROMs as standard built-in equipment in multimedia-related computer platforms and exceed MPC-2 standards using 4X or 6X speed CD-ROMs.

CD-recordable (CD-R) **drives** allow developers to record output on a CD-ROM disk and check how it operates before freezing the design. CD-Rs are also useful as massive recordable storage devices, although it remains economical to produce large quantities of CD-ROM titles using a special mastering and replication service bureau.

CD-ROM titles are undergoing an explosion as interactive games, encyclopedias, and databases proliferate. There are over three dozen CD-ROM drive manufacturers; the major vendors are Apple, Hitachi, NEC, Sony, and Toshiba.

Administering Multimedia Databases

Databases exist as applications based on specific storage concepts. These may consist of data managers, files linked to conventional databases, object databases dedicated to data types, and combinations of these. (Exhibit 4-2 summarizes their characteristics.) Ideally multimedia storage systems contain uncompressed data and a scalable capability—which allows the choice

Exhibit 4-2. Multimedia database categories.

Database Category	Basic Characteristics
Multimedia data managers	Systems that catalog multimedia elements within and outside a computer system
Multimedia storage-embedded systems	Multimedia data types are seen as another Æle within conventional databases that can be manipulated with existing tools.
Hybrid multimedia databases	Includes multimedia data in an object database linked by pointers and descriptors in an RDBMS
Object databases	Designed to store and manipulate binary large objects (BLOBs) of all categories

of compression ratio—for retrieving the information at various levels of compression.

> *Caution:* In practice, this approach is not cost-effective, and as a result, hierarchical storage systems are employed using magnetic, optical, and tape storage devices in various combinations.

▪ *Multimedia data managers* are relatively simple programs that allow users to organize, index, and retrieve objects. They are used to categorize and select elements through the use of descriptors that can be used for retrieval. Some include miniature image displays representative of each object stored; some require language support for manipulation. These tools are designed for the evaluation and selection of objects without relationships to each other or any other data. They are sometimes incorrectly called multimedia databases.

▪ *Multimedia storage-embedded systems* are storage files considered as another field within records in the form of new data types or **binary large objects** (BLOBs), database fields that hold digitized information. This approach makes it possible to manage multimedia files using the existing tools for traditional corporate databases—**relational database management systems**

(RDBMS)—but it is difficult to mix media types and separate elements from RDBMS records. Multimedia files are also subject to all the limitations of traditional files that are not designed to handle multimedia data types.

▪ *Hybrid multimedia storage systems* provide linkage between each multimedia file and a database. Such records include one or more descriptors and pointers (allowing multimedia data to be located at multiple locations) or specialized servers and can be related to other files. This approach requires additional programming tools to synchronize files and ensure transactional integrity. Typical examples are imaging systems, videoservers, and combinations of these.

▪ *Object databases* (ODBs) can store complex, BLOB-like objects as a single entity and allow their manipulation much the same way as data in RDBMSs. ODBs offer a better way to store objects because they provide all of the traditional database services without the overhead of disassembling and reassembling objects whenever they are stored and retrieved. They are ideal as intelligent storage vehicles for multimedia data types. This solution often requires a reorientation of developers used to dealing with conventional RDBMS products. ODBs also come with built-in object-oriented tools and require additional programming knowledge.

Major vendors of RDBMS products with multimedia capabilities include the Ask Group Ingres Division, CINCOM Systems, Empress Software, Hewlett-Packard, IBM, Informix, Oracle, and Sybase. Major original ODB vendors include Object Design, Objectivity, Onto, Servio, UniSQL, and Versant Technology. There are also about two dozen multimedia data manager suppliers, including Aldus, Canto, Delta PoInt, Eastman Kodak, Imspace, IBM, Lenel Systems, and Ravi Technology.

Client-Servers and Video Servers

Client-servers permit information storage and distribution on local networks, allowing PCs and mid-range and mainframe computers to interact with each other on the network. The *client* side of the client-server system provides all facilities relating to the user, such as data and query formats and the way they appear on the screen. The *server* side includes all functions relating to the management and maintenance of data.

Interactive communications within an organization require transmissions of audio and video data streams that can cause a bottleneck and interfere with conventional data traffic, straining the capabilities of client-servers beyond their capacities. One solution is to install a backbone to handle the major traffic and connect users to it directly or through a specialized hub. Another solution is to install multimedia videoservers that do nothing other than store and transmit video data exclusively without interfering with existing network traffic or applications.

A **video server** is a very large storage system that operates like a virtual VCR for a large number of simultaneous users. It is considered to be a crucial concept and a key element in two market segments: collaborative multimedia of the interactive corporation and consumer-interactive TV market segments. Video servers are also playing an important role in customer services, interactive advertising, and kiosk merchandising, both delivered via private networks and available through access to the digital superhighway.

Companies involved in the development of video servers include Novell Multimedia, IBM, Protocomm, Starlight Networks, Oracle Systems, Hewlett-Packard, Silicon Graphics, and Microsoft.

Networks: Key to the Future

The future of multimedia in business depends on interactive networking applications, which also present massive storage, capacity, and network interconnection problems. Existing corporate networks are designed primarily to carry bursty, asynchronous data traffic. Multimedia transmission of audio and video data, in contrast, is a time-sensitive operation requiring continuous and synchronous data transport facilities.

The transmission capacity of existing LANs typically ranges from 10 to 16 Mbps—theoretically more than adequate to support the transmission of audio and video data. However, even a few of these transmissions would rapidly flood a typical LAN, making it unavailable for most other network traffic or causing intolerable delays. Even without the demands of multimedia traffic, corporate LANs are already overloaded due to the rapid growth in data traffic resulting from client-servers and powerful PCs and workstations.

Higher-capacity solutions are being introduced, as well as other switching concepts. Most of these solutions, however, are designed to alleviate the mounting bottlenecks, not to accommodate multimedia networking as such. Among the specific solutions that do address networking, the most promising is **asynchronous transfer mode** (ATM), a high-speed cell-switching technology that can efficiently handle all types of data traffic and has the potential of supporting virtual networks with large transmission capabilities.

The ultimate requirements for multimedia networking are random support for real-time continuous, multiuser, multimedia conferencing and collaborative computing whose bandwidth requirements surpass the capabilities of most corporate networks. Despite the barriers, multimedia networking is *the* solution for implementing a number of corporate functions that include interactive advertising, collaborative computing, multiuser conferencing, concurrent or simultaneous engineering, sales and merchandising programs, corporate training, communications, and administrative functions. Exhibit 4-3 lists examples of application by corporate function.

Building Flexible Operating Systems

During the initial years of multimedia computing, special extensions to DOS, OS/2, and Windows operating systems were required to enable the processing of multimedia applications. Now, the basic multimedia interfacing functions are built into the operating systems, including special features for handling video such as QuickTime or Video for Windows.

For the more powerful 32-bit microprocessors, vendors offer 32-bit operating systems that allow end users to take advantage of the capabilities of the latest PC and workstation

Exhibit 4-3. Multimedia networking applications.

Corporate Function	Multimedia Application
Administration	Multimedia databases, Æle sharing, document imaging, multimedia e-mail, electronic data interchange
Communications	Multimedia conferencing, executive information systems, corporate broadcasting, employee information systems
Manufacturing	Testing procedures, diagnostics, purchasing, equipment maintenance
Marketing	Interactive advertising, promotional presentations, virtual reality simulations, design of commercials, product information kiosks
Product development	Concurrent engineering, product visualizations, design advisers, reference systems, simulations
Sales	Portable multimedia presentations, personal digital assistants, product catalogs, merchandising kiosks, buyers' workstations, selling advisers
Training	Corporate training, management development, just-in-time training, distant training, customer training, sales training

hardware. Nevertheless, 16-bit operating systems are expected to dominate the PC marketplace for some time to come.

The 32-bit operating systems handle twice as many data in the same time and access more data in random access memory (RAM) and disk files than 16-bit operating systems can. End users need not worry about their platform operating system, however, because vendors provide products designed to run on the largest possible number of PCs.

Keep in mind that over half of worldwide operating systems are DOS and Windows products. (See Exhibit 4-4 for other estimates.) According to a recent forecast by Infocorp, this is

Exhibit 4-4. Estimated market shares of operating systems.

Operating System	1995	2000
DOS	25%	20%
Windows 3.0 (16-bit)	10	–
Windows 4.0 (32-bit) Chicago	20	30
Windows NT (32-bit)	2	10
OS/2 (32-bit)	8	12
Macintosh	16	10
UNIX	4	3

Source: Infocorp 1994.

expected to continue through the year 2000, although DOS will lose market share and 16-bit Windows 3.1 will have almost entirely been replaced by 32-bit Windows 95. Keeping in mind that there are already about 60 million Windows users throughout the world, this is an important multimedia platform to keep in mind. For multiuser networked applications, Windows 95, OS/2, and UNIX-based operating systems will be important.

Authoring Systems: Multimedia Catalysts

Authoring systems are the high-level software tools that facilitate the integration of text, graphics, animation, still images, audio, and video into smooth, interactive applications. They are targeted at multimedia creators and designers with little or no computer experience, and they concentrate on presentation content and quality.

The most desirable features for authoring systems are a flexible user interface, the ability to handle full-motion video at TV-broadcast-quality levels, the ability to import as well as create graphics and animation, the introduction of various transitional effects between scenes, the ability to perform branching to selected screens, ready-made buttons for building navigation between scenes, and support of multimedia devices and multiple end-user controls.

More than three dozen authoring systems products are on the market, ranging in cost from $99 to $5,000. Most run under DOS, Windows, or Macintosh operating systems, although some support OS/2, UNIX, Amiga, and NEXTstep. The most popular vendor of authoring systems is Macromedia (with a 30 percent market share estimate). It provides products for Windows and Macintosh. Next is Asymetrix, with its Windows-based ToolBook (20 percent market share estimate), followed by AimTech (10 percent market share) with IconAuthor, which supports Windows, OS/2, and UNIX. Other vendors are Allen Communications, IBM, Network Technology, and Ntergaid.

Microchips:
Small Wonders for Big Solutions

Digitization, compression, and decompression, as well as the display of complex graphics and animation, are information processing functions that are particularly suitable for the development of specialized semiconductor products. In years past, many of these functions were handled by application-specific integrated circuits, but as multimedia computing grew, semiconductor manufacturers introduced digital signal processors (DSPs), specialized microchips that rapidly translate analog signals of the real world into digital patterns that computers can process. In addition DSPs compress and decompress the massive data streams so crucial in handling audio and video in realtime applications.

DSPs were introduced by Intel in 1979 and until recently were supplied primarily to the high-priced military and networking markets. They are also widely used in telecommunications equipment, such as modems, answering machines, and cellular phones. More recent DSP products are designed to operate as coprocessors to provide the building blocks for creating realtime multimedia capabilities that can be built into computers and processing equipment.

DSPs are cost-effective solutions for many multimedia-related data processing functions. They have four major application areas: (1) audio, (2) realtime multimedia, (3) codecs, and (4) compression.

A number of major semiconductor manufacturers are offering multimedia DSPs with varying functions and different capabilities, among them Analog Devices, AT&T, Hewlett-Packard, IBM, Motorola, Texas Instruments, and a number of smaller semiconductor manufacturers.

Texas Instruments believes that the future of multimedia lies in the development of semiconductor products that can handle compression algorithms on a single chip. It has developed the general-purpose multimedia video processor (MVP). These devices, targeted initially at the integrated media workstations market, offer very high resolution, full-motion video, generate graphics and animation, and process input from cameras and video software. Texas Instruments believes that multimedia communications will create a huge demand for MVP-type microchips, particularly for use in imaging and complex document transmission systems.

Delivery and Development Platforms

When you choose a multimedia platform, make sure it conforms to the multimedia PC (MPC) specifications that define minimum hardware and software requirements. Hardware products with the MPC label indicate they meet or exceed minimum MPC specifications set by the Multimedia PC Marketing Council.

The original MPC-1 specification, announced in 1990, is now regarded by industry observers as inadequate for quality multimedia applications. The newer MPC-2 standard extends the original specification, and because many PC products have already surpassed these specifications, the council is developing an MPC-3 standard. The basic parameters of the two standards are outlined in Exhibit 4-5.

There are other platforms too:

- *Apple QuickTime Standard,* a multiplatform solution.
- *IBM Ultimedia Standard,* similar to MPC but supporting the OS/2 operating system.
- *CD-I consumer market platform,* promoted by Philips and Sony.

Exhibit 4-5. Basic MPC platform standards.

Feature	MPC-1	MPC-2
CPU	386SX	486SX, 25 MHz
RAM	2 MB	4 MB
Magnetic storage	3.5-inch HD drive 30 MB hard drive	3.5-inch HD drive 160 MB hard drive
CD-ROM transfer rate	150 KBps	300 KBps
CD-ROM seek time	1 second	400 msec
Video	VGA 640 × 480 × 16 colors	SVGA 640 × 480 × 65,536
Audio sample size	8-bit maximum	16-bit maximum
Audio sample rate	22 KHz maximum	44 KHz maximum

Keyboard, Mouse, and Specialized Peripherals

The MPC specifications define the minimum parameters for multimedia delivery platforms, which basically include CD-ROM drive and speakers (often built into the hardware). In reality, multimedia development platforms should surpass these basic specifications in speed and amount of storage. Also, you will probably need the following peripherals for capturing, digitizing, storing, and distributing multimedia applications:

- *Keyboard and mouse* as standard equipment.
- *Trackballs, light pens, and touch screens,* for developing and deploying special-purpose applications. Touch screens are preferred as interactive control devices for multimedia applications in unattended public areas, such as information or merchandising kiosks.
- *Microphones, audiocassette recorders, or musical instrument digital interface instruments,* for capturing and introducing sounds into the system.
- *Videodisks, video cameras, videotapes, graphic scanners, and digital cameras,* for input of images and moving video. All

audio and video input peripherals require special signal capturing and digitized boards. Many combine various of these functions in a single unit.

- *PC monitor and speakers and headphones,* for output. Headphones are for fine tuning and for environments where sound testing would disturb others. The monitor and speaker are the usual output devices.
- *Videorecorders and CD recorders,* for capturing and mastering the finished product on videotape or CD-ROM disks.
- *Video-camera-equipped PCs,* for conferencing.
- *Multipoint control units,* for videoconferencing.
- *New interfaces, hubs, and switches,* for networked multimedia applications.

Exhibit 4-6 lists these peripherals and shows where they fit in the configuration.

Exhibit 4-6. Peripherals needed for multimedia applications.

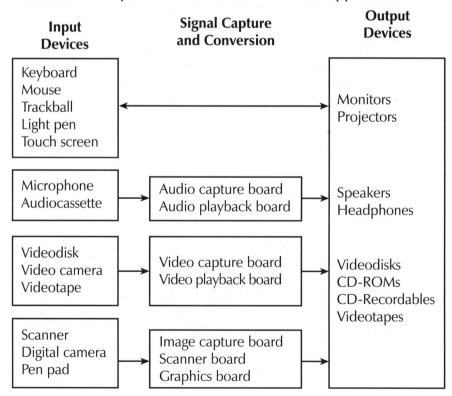

Spotlight on the Future

Industry observers believe that the introduction of interactive multimedia services to increasingly larger numbers of computer-illiterate consumers will result in the development and perfection of voice-activated applications.

Research on realtime interactive multimedia communications conducted by Texas Instruments provides insight into the requirements for achieving realtime networked multimedia traffic as envisaged by virtual LAN concepts and the interactive enterprise. The Texas Instruments findings indicate that full-fledged international multimedia transmissions under the H.261 standard will require hardware capabilities with 1 billion operations per second (BOPS), or about ten times as powerful as the high-end workstations on the market today.

Responding to the challenge, Texas Instruments has developed 2 BOPS MVP devices to integrate video technologies on a single chip. These products use 3 to 4 million transistors and operate at data transfer rates of at least 400 Mbps to ensure smooth realtime transmissions. Current multimedia communications and processing hardware is not yet capable of providing ideal solutions to networking problems. Other semiconductor manufacturers are also developing multimedia microchips to handle audio and video streams more efficiently.

5

How to Implement Multimedia Applications

Multimedia projects involve the integration of hardware, media content, and materials by skilled personnel. In many cases, new expertise outside the traditional information processing environments is needed.

Creativity, aesthetics, and legal factors are not normally part of conventional information processing; but they are significant in multimedia. In the new media environments, content can make or break an application. As a manager you must learn to deal with this new communications universe and include it in your future plans and budgets.

This chapter is important for you to read carefully as you face the challenge of creating and managing multimedia applications. It is also useful if you are purchasing multimedia products and services from the outside.

Charting the Course

In the typical corporate environment, with conventional computing and networking, the manipulation of text and data is almost exclusively under the control of the MIS organization. Its experts produce products of predetermined format, usually dictated by the ultimate end users, who otherwise have little influence on the design and implementation of such systems.

You may be reluctant to become involved with multimedia projects because of the multifaceted integration requirements and the need to deal with unfamiliar issues. Alternative non-multimedia solutions may be tempting but make no mistake: Any other approach will not get you where you want to go.

Here is the way for you to go about this undertaking:

1. Understand the need to integrate multimedia activities into the corporate mainstream.
2. Acquire the know-how to integrate content from various sources into coherent multimedia presentations.
3. Integrate new creative skills into cost-effective development teams.

Preparing to Undertake Multimedia Integration

In traditional data processing, management's job is to deliver systems and services on time and within a budget. The decisions to undertake these projects are, of course, made by top executives, who usually receive recommendations on specific technologies from the more technically oriented and knowledgeable MIS managers. Nevertheless, conventional data processing projects (text and data), aside from different electronic publishing embellishments, look very much alike, so keeping within budget and delivering on time remain the criteria on which the output will be judged.

Multimedia computing and communications is entirely different. Its impact on the end users is more like that of TV and videos, and its justification, even in business, is based on the theory of *hits*—whether users like it. Multimedia applications are judged differently from and with more exacting yardsticks than those applied to conventional information processing projects. These factors must be taken into account during the design stages so that the final product does not bore, alienate, or even offend audiences. This added attention to formats, colors, aesthetics, animation sequences, transitional effects, and other elements increases the time and cost of multimedia development.

Multimedia applications must first be justified as information processing projects of specific corporate value—for example, training, sales, or merchandising. Next, additional creative resources must be added to handle audience-acceptability factors. Other issues are content, knowledge sources, creative skills, permissions and copyrights, aesthetics, and multiple-level integration.

Who Will Handle the Project?

You have several alternative choices as to how to go about installing a system, with the final decision based on organization size, resources, and available skills:

1. *Full-fledged in-house organization.* Handles the complete project.
2. *Mixed mode operation.* Can be done partly in-house and partly using outside consulting organizations.
3. *Outsourcing approach:* Exclusive use of outside experts.
4. *Off-the-shelf purchasing program:* Applications are bought to match the corporate needs of the moment.

Choosing the Approach

The totally in-house operation requires a competent management team with the skills to integrate hardware and content. It probably makes sense in very large corporations with a continuous need to produce, deploy, and maintain multimedia applications. But even the biggest organization may find it more efficient to use an outside consultant with experience in a particular subject.

A mixed mode is the choice of corporations. Project management teams conduct their needs analysis and identify all the resources and skills required. Then they hire outside sources. Smaller companies that need an application but not a continuous effort can benefit by outsourcing the complete project, including the need analysis. A large number of small development shops exist. The challenge is to select and evaluate the one best suited to the company's needs.

The last alternative, off-the-shelf programs, is primarily for small firms or organizations that are unlikely to develop in-house skills or project management teams (e.g., hospitals). Off-the-shelf applications cover general topics like management, health care, electrical skills, and software development. Titles are available on CD-ROMs, and the only equipment needed are PCs with CD-ROM drives.

Development Steps

Each of these solutions has its own steps to go through over the course of the project:

In-house Multimedia Development

1. Develop the project management team.
2. Identify target audiences.
3. Develop specifications.
4. Identify and select multimedia hardware.
5. Identify and select authoring and editing software.
6. Identify multimedia content sources.
7. Determine legal and permission issues.
8. Organize integration teams.
9. Conduct application testing and deployment.
10. Provide for maintenance and updating.

Mixed Multimedia Development Activity

1. Establish project management team.
2. Conduct a needs analysis.
3. Identify specific skills required.
4. Identify and evaluate outside consultants.
5. Establish application specifications.
6. Contract specific skills to implement project.

Outsourcing All Multimedia Development

1. Establish multimedia project management.
2. Identify multimedia applications.
3. Select and evaluate outside multimedia consultants.
4. Develop contract specifications.
5. Award and monitor consulting project performance.

Acquiring Existing Multimedia Products

1. Identify multimedia requirements.
2. Identify multimedia products on the market.

3. Select and evaluate multimedia titles.
4. Test comparative multimedia products on target audiences.
5. Acquire, deploy, and update multimedia applications.

Target Your Audiences

Multimedia development projects give special attention to end users. Potential audiences are studied and their characteristics determined, so that the approach will maximize appeal to them. Factors not normally taken into account in technology must also be considered in assessing audiences. Among them are size of user groups, frequency of system use, and motivation. Characteristics of individual users—age, education, competence level, and profession—are important too. This audience analysis yields vital information that influences platform selection, so it needs to be undertaken during the needs analysis, at the project's outset.

Identify Your Knowledge Sources

Media content sources should be identified during the needs analysis phase to ensure that the needed materials and documents are available and to determine ownership of materials so that rights and permissions can be obtained.

Many media elements are available in electronic form or are suitable for computer processing via input devices (scanners, video recorders, digital cameras, microphones) and software that captures, edits, compresses, and stores data in digital form. Usable materials may exist in corporate promotion, audiovisual, advertising, public relations, art, and training departments. If these resources are not available in-house, outside sources can provide them. Possible sources are professional stock houses for photographs, films, and videos; publishers of books and magazines; museums and universities; professional associations; and government agencies. Additional time and funds may have to be budgeted for outside sources.

See Exhibit 5-1 for a listing of sources, inside and outside the organization.

Exhibit 5-1. Media content sources inside and outside the organization.

Category	Description of Source
Internal	Corporate directories and manuals
	Corporate advertising
	Public relations
	Promotional and marketing materials
	Product usage and maintenance
	Executive speeches–audiotapes
	Annual reports–print or video
	Corporate art department
	Computer graphics resources
	Electronic publishing
	Training department
	Product and systems experts
External	Stock music and sound effects
	Stock images and photographs
	Stock Ælms and videos
	Publishing organizations
	Newspaper morgues
	Broadcasting organizations
	Public and private libraries
	Research organizations
	Government agencies
	Rights and permissions associations
	Universities
	Museums
	Software multimedia programs
	Expert consultants
	Other corporations

Consult the Legal Eagles

Because multimedia is relatively new, the legality of many of its aspects is still being tested. Some attorneys claim that even some methods of presentation may be patentable.

All content materials—illustrations, literature quotations, movies, video clips, documentaries, market data, music, and software—are protected by copyrights. Content material may come from corporate files, but that does not mean that rights and permissions for use are automatic. Corporate materials previously used and purchased from outside sources may have restrictions. Because these applications are more visible than conventional information systems, there is an increased probability that unauthorized use will be noticed, resulting in costly and time-consuming legal action. Additionally, permission must be obtained from anyone whose image, voice, or artwork will be used.

If the materials were developed by employees or outside vendors for the organization, chances are that the organization owns the material. Nevertheless, it is still wise to consult the legal department.

All legal aspects should be considered during the needs analysis phase.

Acquiring the Technical Know-How

Pick the Platform That Delivers

There are two platform categories pertaining to the development and delivery of applications:

1. *Development platforms,* fast and powerful PCs or workstations with adequate storage and a complement of the peripheral devices to capture, digitize, compress, and produce an integrated multimedia application.
2. *Delivery platforms,* with delivery accomplished in a number of ways depending on the audience and application objectives. In stand-alone mode, a delivery platform could be an upgraded PC or portable laptop, and notebooks. The more practical way to look at delivery platforms is by function: Select the best hardware to meet the defined needs. The other way is to look at existing multimedia platform standards and assess specific value to particular application.

In choosing a platform to support a specific function, make sure the proposed application can run on it. In most cases, platforms exist to support other productivity or operational functions and will need upgrading to handle multimedia. The exception is a merchandising kiosk network or the deployment of portable platforms for a sales force designed to promote and sell specific products or services. Exhibit 5-2 summarizes this approach to the platform selection issue.

The MPC-1– and MPC-2–compliant PCs constitute the largest population of users and undoubtedly represent the safest choice, but the MPC-3 standard platform is already making headway, underscoring an important point: Always take into consideration the latest available standards. Choosing the latest standard represents an advantage because there will always be the greatest selection of the most advanced third-party software tools and multimedia titles available. Exhibit 5-3 summarizes the major multimedia platform standards and predominant applications.

Consider Upgrading Your Hardware

Probably the best way to create multimedia platforms and protect your initial investment in hardware and software is to upgrade your existing PCs. Upgrading can be accomplished by buying multimedia hardware and software components and integrating them into the existing PC equipment or by purchasing ready-made upgrade kits.

Upgrade kits usually include an audio board, CD-ROM drive, and software titles that allow immediate exploration of the upgrades' audio and video capabilities. The advantage to these kits is that additional hardware is matched and tested to operate smoothly on predetermined PCs, so you are not burdened with testing and adjusting suitable hardware components. Nevertheless, multimedia upgrading is a complex procedure; the safest solution is to have it installed by a dealer who guarantees performance.

At least a dozen MPC-2 upgrade kit vendors with about thirty products are available. Kits vary in capabilities and range in price from $400 to more than $1,500.

Upgrading existing hardware may be desirable, but keep

Exhibit 5-2. Selection criteria for multimedia platforms.

Delivery Mode	Best Multimedia Platforms
Stand-alone PCs	PC, Macintosh, or Amiga platforms with built-in or upgradable multimedia capabilities, including CD-ROMs, speakers, and audio and video boards
Networked PCs	PC, Macintosh, or UNIX workstations with multimedia capabilities as for stand-alone PCs. CD-ROM drives could be an option if client servers or video servers are used to store and distribute multimedia applications.
Merchandising kiosks	Specialized multimedia networks usually based on lowest-cost platforms for operation through touch screens by random and unpredictable publics. Use of low-end PCs, Macintosh, or CD-I platforms is most common.
Portable platforms	Mostly PC laptops and notebooks equipped with CD-ROMs or special CD-ROM players with limited computing capabilities.
Groupware	Networked PCs and UNIX workstations with sufÆcient speed and storage capabilities to operate in collaborative environments, simultaneously sharing data, Æles, whiteboards, voice, and fax.
Videoconferencing	Point-to-point or multipoint networked PCs, Macintosh, or UNIX platforms equipped with video cameras and special videoconferencing interfaces using high-speed or analog communication lines

Exhibit 5-3. Multimedia platform standards and applications.

Platform Standard	Predominant Applications
MPC-1, MPC-2	Most popular PC and compatibles standard, with largest percentage of PC population using DOS and Windows operating systems. Basic delivery platform for stand-alone, portable, and corporate networked environments.
QuickTime	Apple Macintosh platforms popular in electronic publishing, advertising, and TV production. Older models of Macintosh platforms do not provide color displays. QuickTime standard is now being ported to Windows and other platforms.
CD-I	A Philips and Sony consumer electronics standard that is often used as a low-cost delivery platform in business environments.
Amiga	Excellent graphics and video capabilities with about 6 million users worldwide, but Commodore withdrew from the microcomputer business in April 1994. Support for Amiga platforms in the future is questionable, and available software is limited relative to other standards.
CD-ROM players	Portable devices designed for consumer and business markets. Limited to multimedia presentations for sales forces and video games and other entertainment products. Provides playback without computing capabilities.
IBM Ultimedia	OS/2-based platform comparable to MPC-2 designed for multimedia development and delivery on high-end PCs, RISC workstations, and AS 400 minicomputers. Compatible with DOS and Windows multimedia platforms.
UNIX	High-performance networked platform in engineering and scienti/Ec applications. Many versions of UNIX make cross-platform usage highly questionable but Novell is developing a more common UNIX operating version to alleviate this problem.

in mind that PCs are only marginally more expensive and they are considerably faster. The best multimedia PCs are now based on the fastest Pentium processors, which come with the basic audio boards and CD-ROMs.

Integrate the Hardware Without Hassle

Transforming a microcomputer into a multimedia development or delivery platform is accomplished by combining a variety of hardware products into an integrated system. This means selecting, acquiring, testing, operating, and maintaining audio and video hardware and matching it with conventional computer equipment. If you are not familiar with these products or their sources, part of your job will be learning the criteria necessary to evaluate and select the hardware.

Hardware integration differs according to whether a multimedia development facility is being established or existing desktops and networks are being converted into multimedia-capable delivery platforms and systems. In the latter situation, hardware integration is relatively simple. It involves upgrading existing platforms with CD-ROMs or laserdisks, speakers, and appropriate audio and video boards to handle the playback.

If you are establishing a facility, the hardware integration is more complex because you will have to integrate hardware devices that provide original audio and video inputs, animation, text, and data, as well as smooth transitions between different segments. This task requires specialized experience in audio and video hardware and information technology and means taking time to evaluate a great number and variety of special peripheral devices and programs. Moreover, because of rapid technological changes, you will have to keep track of all types of input and output devices necessary to meet emerging needs. The most cost-effective solutions today are to buy an integrated multimedia system with the appropriate software and peripherals.

Meet the Challenges of Media Content Integration

Content integration is a greater challenge than hardware integration to managers used to handling conventional data (text and numbers). Complex data sets representing voice, images, animation, and motion video elements must be synchronized, compressed, transmitted, and displayed at speeds comparable to those of broadcast TV. Production is usually a trade-off among output quality, development speed, and price, though quality of output is the critical factor.

Some managers may not be as concerned as media professionals are with output quality, but never forget that output quality makes or breaks the application. The aesthetics employed by the most successful applications manipulate end users toward making the most productive decisions. In practical terms, this means that development projects must give special attention to content integration from the outset.

Another aspect of this task is source identification for content and data. This necessitates familiarity with data managers, databases, and object databases that handle multimedia data sets. You need to identify new data sources or media elements and convert them to electronic form available with your hardware.

Developing Your Project Team

Identify the Creative Talent

Multimedia sources are driven by creativity. Apple, IBM, and Microsoft know that creative talent comes from corporate cultures other than those in information technology. You must take the time to seek out and identify creative people capable of designing and developing multimedia applications. Typically the following people are required on a multimedia project:

Producer	Responsible for content and effective communication to target audiences; coordinates all people and tasks between creative and authoring staff; develops budget and manages development.

Production assistant	Develops and tracks schedules and coordinates details; lines up specialized skills when required; investigates content sources.
Project administrator	Responsible for business aspects of the project (e.g., contracts, purchase orders, user approval, permissions).
Interactive designer	Develops storyboard and general look; conceives user interfaces, branching, looping, performance measurement, graphics, and colors; interprets design into a decision tree or flowchart.
Scriptwriter	Acts as editor and reduces all input to a final script delivering the intended messages; develops words for storyboard and video.
Graphics producer	Details individual screens with specific menus, animation, navigation, and interactive content for ease of operation by end users.
Image capture specialist (usually a freelance contractor)	Captures and digitizes original images or documents and photographs.
Video producer	Plans, manages, and supervises original video shooting for the project.
Audio engineer	Responsible for recording narrative and digitizing audio materials for use in the application; acquires outside music and audio materials.
Author, programmer	Responsible for linking all multimedia elements based

	on decision tree, storyboards, and scripts sequenced into interactive application.
Content expert	End-user or client specialist who advises production staff during design and development on accuracy of content.
System tester	Samples end users or target audiences for feedback on parts of the system as these are being developed.

Content and sequences must be designed to appeal to the majority of the audience so the aesthetics—the artistic result—provides a satisfying experience for end users. The responsibility of MIS management is to focus on user preferences in order to deliver the most effective application.

Take on the Biggest Challenge: Integrating Human Skills

Probably the most challenging task is the successful merging of the opinions and talents of information processing specialists, knowledge engineers, and multimedia creative types (art directors, film producers, graphics and video experts, advertising executives, educational psychologists, and training specialists). Artists, writers, and animators do not always respond to managerial techniques in the same way as other corporate employees do. Leading and inspiring disparate types and molding them into a smoothly working development team can be the toughest challenge of all.

Any multimedia implementation and skills integration requires a large number of trade-offs between quality of the finished products and budgetary and administrative constraints. Realize at the outset that when content makes or breaks the application, quality of output becomes the most critical issue, and only the proper mix and creative management of skills can ensure that it will take place.

Project Management Process

Precise planning is difficult considering the number of information sources and variety and number of players needed to create a multimedia application. Therefore, an organized effort designed to proceed in a flexible and documented manner through all stages—needs analysis, design, development, testing and validation, maintenance, and updating—is most important. Exhibit 5-4 sets out this process.

Needs analysis is particularly valuable to information technology or MIS specialists who have not been involved with creative aspects. The needs analysis should be undertaken before any funding or delivery commitments are made. It should in-

Exhibit 5-4. Project management methodology.

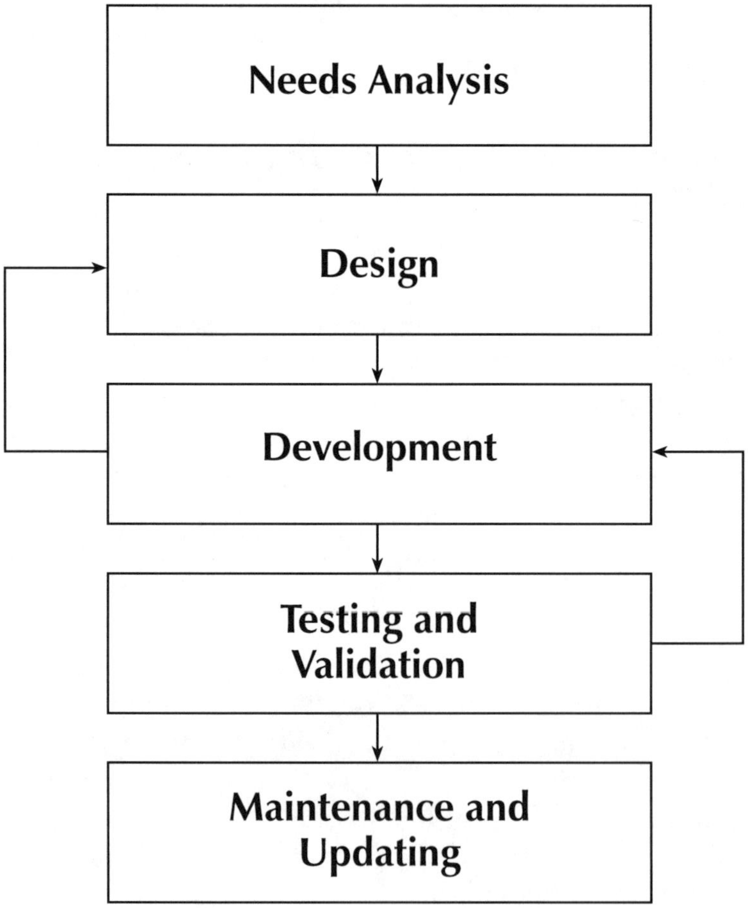

clude a clear definition of the objectives, an extensive appraisal of the audiences, and assessment of the delivery environment, because it determines the operational parameters within the application.

> Critical point: If networked transactions are being planned, make sure there is sufÆcient bandwidth to handle trafÆc without degradation of networking operations.

The Planning Stage and After

Once needs analysis uncovers all the requirements and limitations within the application, it is time to develop cost and time estimates and formalize the conceptual design in the form of a **storyboard** that outlines the presentation highlights.

Overall application development is best completed and documented with a decision tree flowchart relating individual screens to each other and identifying all interactivity built into the system. The decision tree is like a map that all team members can use to understand specific roles and to measure progress. Exhibit 5-5 illustrates such a decision tree.

Once all planning activities are complete, it is time to determine the most useful authoring systems and software development tools that should be used to build and test the system. Project development from then on becomes a continuous process of trade-offs between quality of output and available resources. The final necessary step is a maintenance provision that allows users to obtain prompt assistance.

Exhibit 5-5. Project decision tree concept.

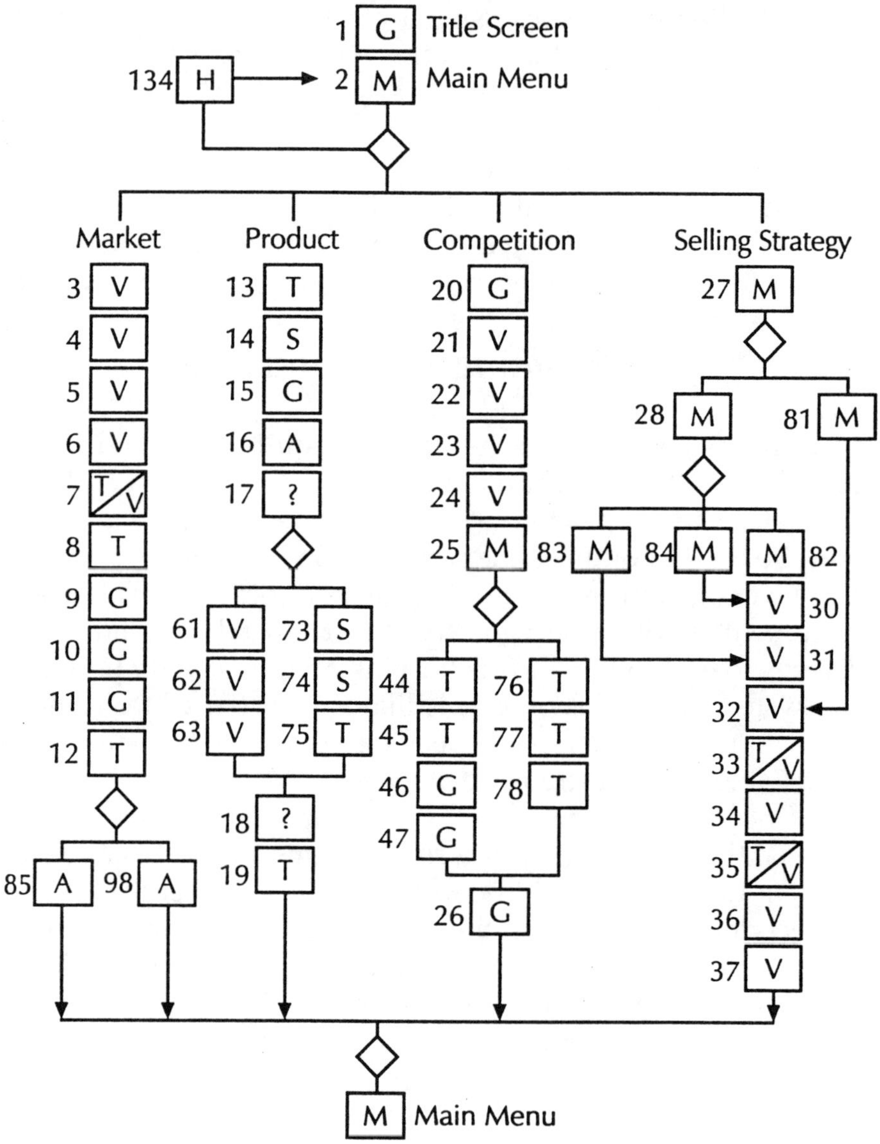

Note:
An interactive multimedia program is produced by stringing together screens (identified by numbers) in a sequential order.

Key:

A	Animation	S	Still image	◻	Overlay screen
G	Text and graphics	T	Text only	?	Question screen
H	Help screen	V	Video only	◇	Branching point
M	Menu				

6

When You Choose to Upgrade Your Existing Information Systems

If you are upgrading an existing system, your first focus is the applications you need if you are to remain competitive; the second consideration is what your existing system's infrastructure can handle. At this point, MIS managers and business managers must agree on customer service functions and how the company generates profit. Functions contributing to profits must be tackled first. Applications that provide better consumer support and differentiate your company from the competition are the most likely to benefit from multimedia.

Is Your Equipment Adequate?

Investments in **legacy technology**—an information system that has been in existence for a long time—may be causing a slowdown in new application implementation. Yet managers are reluctant to rip out existing systems and reinvest in new—and unpredictable—technologies.

> Note this: Resistance is understandable but not always advisable.

Modern multimedia, however, demands storage, transmission, and display infrastructures that are more demanding than those of conventional information systems. The introduction of corporate groupware applications, desktop videoconferencing, and access to the World Wide Web and an explosion of mobile multimedia platforms suggest that multimedia applications are on the increase. Traditional database management systems, though, are seldom multimedia capable or upgradable. Many corporations are considering multimedia as they reengineer systems and introduce new client-server operating environments.

Multimedia applications for the most part are stand-alone PCs. Adopters are exploring new ways to incorporate multimedia into existing systems.

Phasing In Multimedia Capabilities

Because of the size of the investment, upgrading can be performed in four phases over a period of years and synchronized with reengineering and training.

Phase 1: Bridging data gaps	Development of internal multimedia information delivery applications, including storage, retrieval, and store-and-forward transmissions
Phase 2: Front-line sales and marketing support	Development of multimedia presentations and mobile platforms in sales and marketing environments to improve interaction with existing and potential clients
Phase 3: Extended enterprise concept	Development of interactive multimedia communications with business partners, suppliers, and clients, leading toward operation of a virtual corporation
Phase 4: Multimedia cyberspace operations	Extension of interactive multimedia communications capa-

bilities to Internet and World Wide Web and providing linkage with interactive TV networks

The duration of each phase differs from corporation to corporation, depending on each one's size and competitive environment.

Phase 1: Bridging Data Gaps

In phase 1, the need to develop internal corporate multimedia capabilities is immediate. Either existing storage, retrieval, and data transmission facilities can be upgraded or new, specialized hardware and software can be added.

In a typical enterprise, traditional systems provide integrity, security, and management for all kinds of corporate data, mostly in text and number form. The highly structured RDBMS products, however, are not ideal for very large files representing voice, video, graphics, and animation. As a result, vendors are adding object-oriented capabilities to existing RDBMS products to meet two objectives: (1) to protect the huge investment in systems their clients already have and (2) to provide storage, retrieval, and transmission capabilities within existing informations.

Sybase, an early database supplier, recognized multimedia's importance and developed Gain Momentum products to provide it with development, storage, and retrieval capabilities. Other vendors, such as Oracle and Informix, developed specific data handling capabilities and specialized video servers for manipulation of realtime audio and video data. Starlight Networks provides specialized video server software and hardware products for upgrading existing information systems and networks.

Phase 2: Sales and Marketing Support

Once corporate information systems are equipped with multimedia handling capabilities, sales and support personnel can take full advantage of the applications.

Advantage: Sales and marketing activities are enhanced by tools that improve customer interaction and productivity.

Initially the applications may be the stand-alone implementations developed simultaneously with upgraded information systems. When sufficient transmission capacity is available, these sales and marketing systems can operate online, linked directly to the corporation information system.

A good idea: Proceed with the development of interactive multimedia sales and marketing applications even if corporate information systems are not fully multimedia capable.

Once applications are developed, they become an asset even on a stand-alone basis and can always be linked to legacy systems later.

Now is the time to check out the possibilities: interactive CD-ROMs, laptop and notebook computers, specialized CD-ROM players, hand-held digital organizers, and networking possibilities that include digital wireless systems.

Phase 3: The Extended Enterprise

The extended enterprise phase—interaction with customers, suppliers, business partners, and financial organizations—becomes possible when work groups can instantly connect up into a realtime multimedia conferencing network. Desktop videoconferencing and multiuser collaborative conferencing systems can be introduced independently to enhance communications among parties before they become part of an overall network.

Tip: Make sure systems are expandable and compatible with developing networks.

Public-access twenty-four-hour merchandising kiosks are an interim stage and can be designed to operate as self-contained networks. These kiosks eventually must be linked up to systems containing the basic customer and market information.

Phase 4: Moving Into Cyberspace

The final phase of corporate multimedia improvements reaches into cyberspace with interconnecting WANs, third-party video-conferencing services, WWW servers, **home pages,** and interactive TV. Access and entry into cyberspace must be easy and secure.

Corporations rushing to establish a WWW presence with information systems that are not ready for interconnectivity should make sure that adequate **firewalls** are built between existing networks and the outside cyberspace to protect it from electronic raids. Exhibit 6-1 illustrates a firewall installation. Companies may develop multimedia applications first on corporation intranets before allowing connectivity with the public and the wide-open Internet.

How to Combine Legacy and Multimedia Data Types

The problem in upgrading legacy systems with multimedia capabilities is how to combine data in traditional RDBMSs with multimedia data containing huge files of audio, video, graphics, and animation. Suppliers, however, offer a variety of solutions. Computer Associates incorporates 3-D graphics and virtual reality in its CA-Unicenter/The Next Generation software. IBM is field-testing an object-oriented Cobol system that includes a VisualSet compiler and programming language targeted at end users with major investments in mainframe systems. PowerPoint for Windows 95's tools are streamlined with a user interface and powerful multimedia enhancements. The software takes full advantage of the multimedia features built in and can work with the Media Player application. This support includes the ability to place video clips precisely on slides. PowerPoint 95 offers slide presentation sound effects. Compact disc soundtracks and audio files can be converted to more efficient formats to save storage space. Animation has special ef-

Exhibit 6-1. A firewall to protect information.

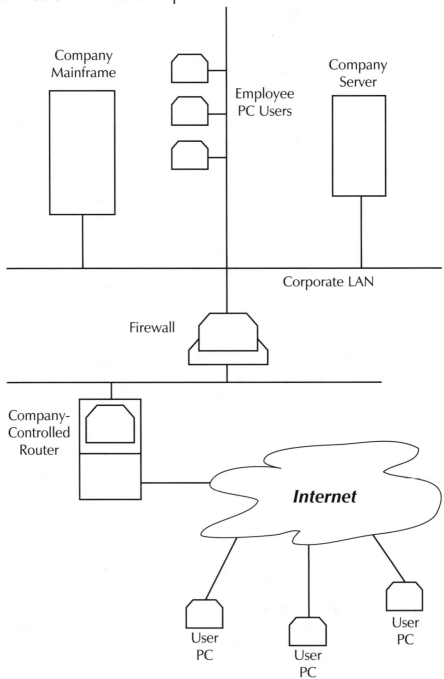

fects, including sounds for artwork. An additional feature is the Meeting Minder, to track action notes and minutes of a meeting during a presentation. Other facilities allow compilation of files in portable format for use on one or more diskettes.

Helpful Object-Oriented Concepts

Many new multimedia-capable software tools are object oriented; each element can be treated as a separate self-contained object. Once mainframe users use object-oriented software, it becomes simple to introduce multimedia content.

Some vendors offer add-on features to allow object data to be stored alongside conventional RDBMS data. Object-relational databases are the wave of the future. Computer Associates, Oracle, and Sybase are the leading vendors.

Graphic User Interfaces

The GUI allows information technology workers to operate more efficiently by freeing them from the use of text and unintelligible commands. GUIs use icons, graphic images, and text to represent and describe procedures or actions. They are thus transitional facilities toward fully interactive multimedia. They are productive and useful operating interfaces that provide a measure of security.

Intelligent Advisory Systems

Reengineering and staff reductions mean that remaining employees take on added responsibilities. To facilitate decision making, it may be necessary to empower them with intelligent multimedia advisory systems and simultaneous access to information still residing in the legacy or information systems.

In the past, solutions have been implemented by using expert systems based on artificial intelligence. Now these same expert systems can be enhanced with multimedia content to become intelligent advisers. In some cases, authoring tools include **inferencing engines** (the processing program in an expert system) which permit the development of cost-effective intelligent multimedia advisers.

Video Servers

Improved RDBMSs may be able to handle some multimedia data but are inadequate to manipulate highly time-sensitive video materials that cause bottlenecks in corporate networks. Where video is being manipulated and stored, the best solution is a video server operating parallel with other data servers. This assumes sufficient transmitting capacity in networks. A typical video server function is illustrated in Exhibit 6-2.

Networks

The effect of interactive multimedia communications on existing networks depends on the requirements of a particular application. Some implementations can run on traditional networks without undue delays or notable degradation in quality of video transmissions. Nevertheless, do not be lulled into complacency. A 10-Mbps **Ethernet** (the most widely used LAN access method) can support three or four realtime videoconferences if screen sizes are small, image refresh rates are low, and the regular network traffic is excluded. Even so, with full screen images and broadcast-TV quality of 30 fps, much more capacity will be needed, particularly when dealing with prospects and clients who will surely be exposed to competitive presentations and transmissions.

Interactive multimedia networking capability is a mission-critical requirement of future communications environments. This means increasing the LAN and WAN bandwidth either selectively or globally to handle anticipated multimedia and conventional data traffic simultaneously.

Several alternatives are available for upgrading existing networks. Some involve architectural changes in network configuration such as **segmentation,** whereby individual users are provided with a higher-bandwidth capability than normal. Exhibit 6-3 illustrates LAN segmentation to accommodate multimedia traffic with minimum delays and deterioration but at an added cost.

There are other alternatives as well. One is isochronous

Exhibit 6-2. Function of a multimedia video server.

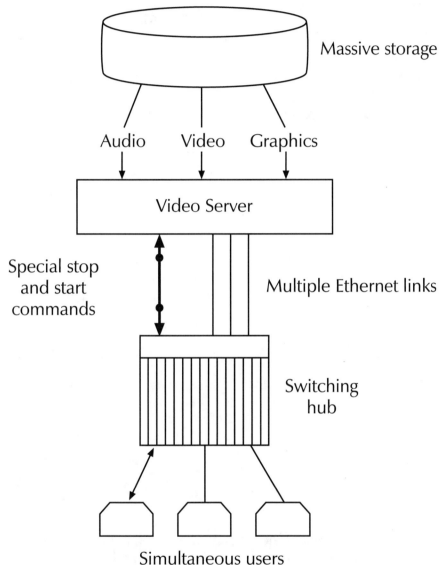

Ethernet (isoENET), which increases existing Ethernet capacity, is dedicated to video and audio transmission, and runs on existing wires.

Be aware: These solutions boost existing LAN capabilities and protect corporate investments for a while, but they

Exhibit 6-3. LAN segmentation upgrading alternative.

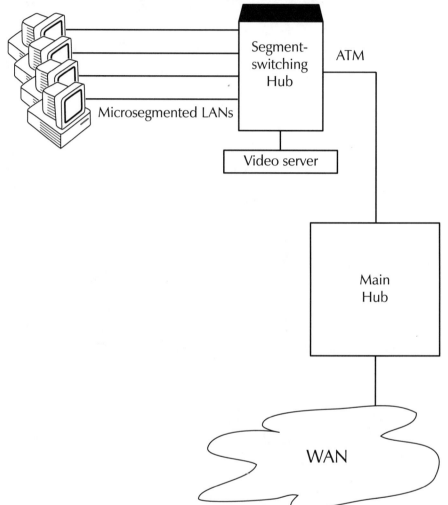

require additional funding, may mean delays in transmissions, require special hubs and interfaces, and are usually only temporary.

Other choices—fiber distributed data interface (FDDI), copper distributed data interface (CDDI), and fast Ethernet—are more expensive and radical but provide 100 Mbps bandwidth capacity to the desktop. And asynchronous transfer mode delivers up to 155 Mbps using fiber-optic cable.

All solutions require new adapter cards, LAN switches, or hubs. Exhibit 6-4 summarizes upgrading alternatives.

Exhibit 6-4. Multimedia network upgrading alternatives.

Networking Alternatives		Description and Comments
Existing LANs	Ethernet segmentation	Individual LAN users are provided with high-bandwidth segments up to 10 Mbps Ethernet capacity
	isoENET	Existing Ethernet LAN capacity is increased by additional 6 Mbps, dedicated exclusively to audio and video transmissions
	Fast Ethernet	Existing LANs enhanced with hubs, switches to handle multimedia trafÆc on a priority basis with up to 100 Mbps bandwidth capacity
New networks	Fiber distributed data interface (FDDI)	100 Mbps optical Æber networks not suitable for realtime interactive video
	Copper distributed data interface (CDDI)	100 Mbps FDDI concept implemented on copper wires with limited range
	Asynchronous transfer mode (ATM)	Up to 155 Mbps bandwith capacity possible at the desktop using Æber-optic cables considered ideal for realtime interactive multimedia transmissions

In choosing high-speed LAN technologies to upgrade information systems, price, **latency** (the time between initiating a request for data and the beginning of the data transfer), and image quality—as well as characteristic trade-offs—must be considered. Multimedia transmissions are particularly vulnerable to latency because large files are bandwidth intensive. The 100 Mbps LAN technologies provide adequate bandwidth to support store-and-forward multimedia transmissions within a corporate LAN, but do not always maintain multiuser realtime interactive collaborative work.

Only FDDI and ATM mechanisms guarantee bandwidth. Of the two, ATM is the better networking solution. Once infra-

Exhibit 6–5. Asynchronous transfer mode data transmission concept.

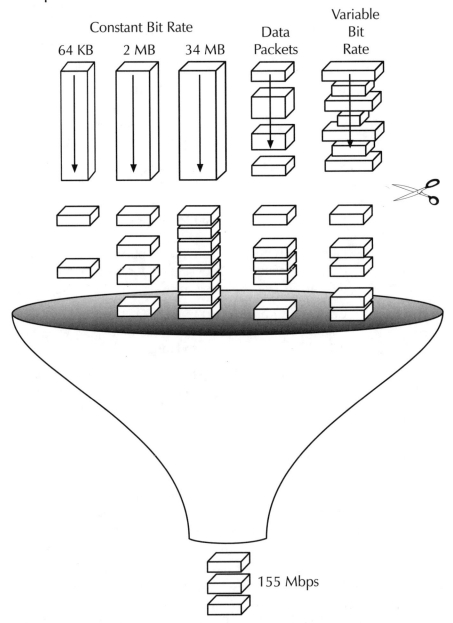

Source: Computer Technology Research Corporation, "Multimedia Networking and Communications."

structures are in place, connectivity and availability of multimedia applications within the information systems will accelerate. ATM provides up to 155 Mbps of bandwidth and supports audio, video, and data transmissions simultaneously. It is the only technology that can reserve bandwidth for audio and video while transmitting data. ATM is also best for realtime video despite its cost. Product prices, however, are declining rapidly. Exhibit 6-5 illustrates the ATM and its ability to handle multimedia data transmission.

7

Multimedia Conferencing: Management Tool of the Future

Desktop videoconferencing products are not perfect. The communications links are often inadequate and video quality is poor, but better and cheaper products are being designed and produced daily.

Desktop videoconferencing, particularly the multiuser variety that exploits existing telephone lines and LANs, is a powerful management tool when efficiently used. This is particularly true in applications such as customer service, telemarketing, and remote business negotiations.

PC vendors offer desktop audio- and video-ready platforms at reasonable prices. In many instances, the end user does not have to configure the desktop to operate with videoconferencing products because they are already bundled with appropriate hardware and software.

Projections of desktop videoconferencing shipments suggest an explosion accelerated by dropping prices and mounting competition among videoconferencing vendors. According to Personal Technology Research 86,000 units were shipped in 1995; the projection for 1998 is a whopping 5.2 million units. Infonetics Research predicts that desktop videoconferencing will become the second most popular multimedia application by 1998 after corporate training and business presentations which compete for the top spot today.

Conferencing Systems

Multimedia Conferencing

Properly implemented multimedia conferencing, an extension of traditional videoconferencing systems and services, presents advantages to corporations that can implement it within work groups, projects, or on an enterprise-wide basis. One of the most obvious is a reduction of travel expenses. Others are less tangible. For example, videoconferencing increases information retention by 50 percent and accelerates buying decisions by 77 percent. These results are derived from psychological research, which suggests that during person-to-person meetings, spoken words convey only 7 percent of the intended meaning. Intonation is responsible for another 38 percent and visual cues contribute as much as 55 percent.

> Payoff: In a multimedia conferencing environment, such factors can be optimized, leading to a more predictable and controllable meeting outcome.

Cost-cutting and productivity benefits can be realized as well in training, telecommuting, job interviewing, medical consulting, distance learning, and customer services. Videoconferencing can reduce travel costs and accelerate the time required to reach a consensus. Videoconferencing between business partners and customers requires access to public networks or videoconferencing services in addition to high-bandwidth private networks, and costs are higher. Exhibit 7-1 compares travel costs with videoconferencing costs.

In evaluating videoconferencing costs, you must take into account the amount of time used on an average day and the associated transmission costs. If daily usage falls below three hours, switched services, such as an integrated services digital network or switched digital services, are preferable because charges are made on a per-call basis. If videoconferencing is

Exhibit 7-1. Comparative videoconferencing costs.

Cost Factors	Specific Parameters to Be Considered
Travel costs	■ Number of people traveling ■ Travel time × average salaries ■ Miles traveled × mileage rate ■ Plane fares, airport access and parking ■ Auto rental and insurance
Per-diem Expenses	■ Hotels and motels ■ Meals ■ Incidentals ■ Rental of presentation equipment
Compared with Videoconferencing	
Audio transmission	■ Service charges ■ Distance-based transmission charge ■ Microphones and speakers
Video transmission	■ Origination facility charge ■ Video session production cost ■ Receiving site charges ■ Transmission costs ■ Multiuser control units

conducted for more than three hours per day, dedicated lines and long-term discounts on virtual private networks are more cost-effective. Exhibit 7-2 summarizes this information.

Distance between parties using videoconferencing systems is also a factor. As distance increases, so does the cost of travel, and videoconferencing becomes more justifiable. The number of participants is also a cost factor, but there is a point of diminishing return beyond six to eight users at different locations. It is difficult to schedule simultaneous videoconferences for larger groups. The costs of multiuser control units between dissimilar videoconferencing equipment may be prohibitive.

Traditional Videoconferencing

Original videoconferencing systems date back to the early 1980s and are expected to remain in use for some time to come.

Exhibit 7-2. Videoconferencing usage frequency factor.

Daily Usage Rate	Preferred Videoconferencing Solution
Less than 3 hours	Integrated Services Digital Network (ISDN) or switched digital services are more cost effective because charges can be made on a per-call basis
Over 3 hours	Dedicated T-1 lines or virtual private networks are more cost-effective as a result of set monthly fees and long-term discounts
Number of users	ISDN access is cheaper if fewer than eight users will be using videoconferencing for 1 hour each day

For this type of conferencing, the participants gather in a specific conference room equipped as a videoconference transmission and reception center. A movable videoconferencing system that can be wheeled to a conference room is known as a **rollabout system**. It is linked through transmission networks and modems with another permanent or mobile facility of the same type.

A facility of this type is based on video compression and decompression devices (codecs) that permit realtime, full-motion, color video transmissions over facilities ranging in bandwidth from 56 Kbps to 2.048 Mbps. Participants can transmit video, audio, data, and graphics over a single digital line using cameras, microphones, scanners, and special network access devices. Exhibit 7-3 shows these elements. The codec is the central device in these systems, as the exhibit illustrates. It receives all analog signals from local cameras and microphones and converts them to digital signals for transmission through an appropriate network access device. It also converts received digital signals to analog and transmits them to the local monitors and speakers.

The camera, located above or next to the monitor pointing at the conference table, can be adjusted using pan, tilt, zoom, and focus controls located on the control panel of the system. Other controls adjust speaker volume and select input devices for feeding signals to the remote site. Microphones are distrib-

Exhibit 7-3. Elements of a videoconferencing system.

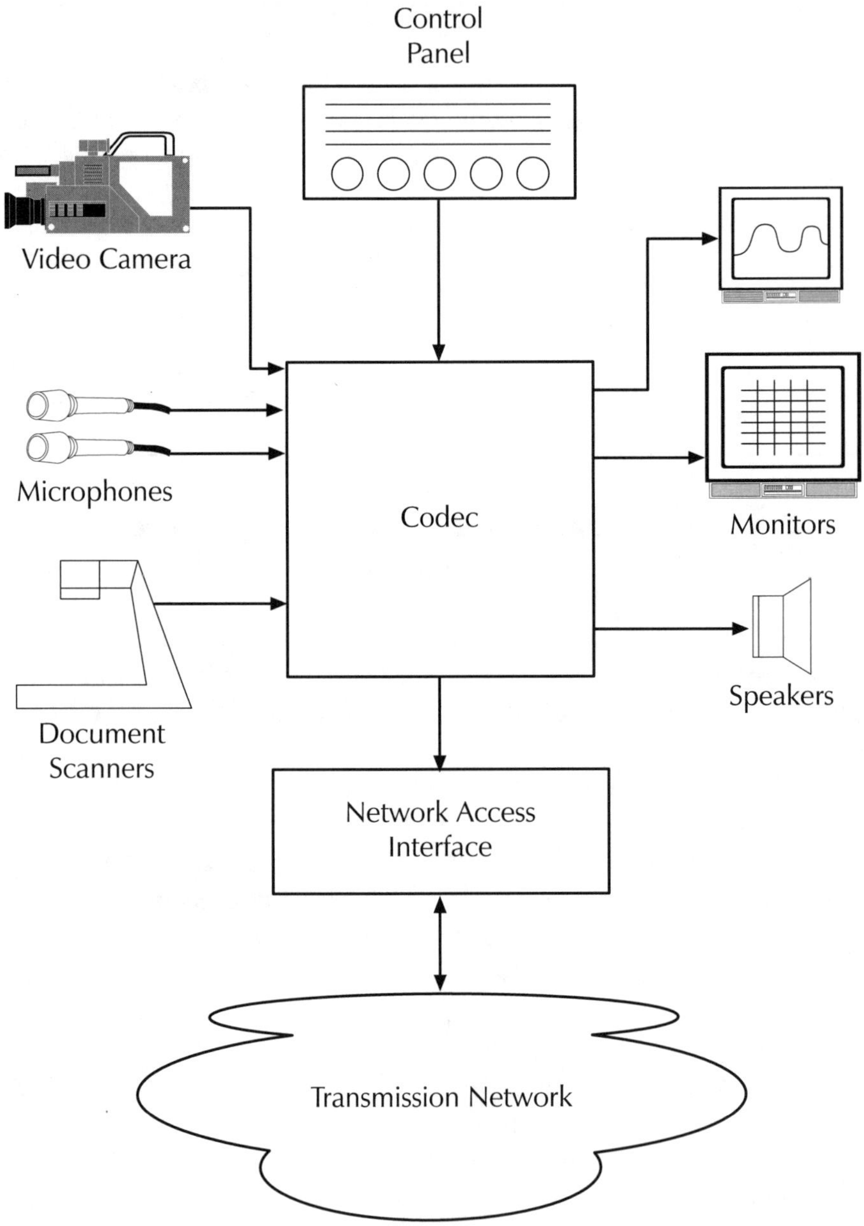

uted around the conference table and can be disconnected indi-
vidually to allow private conversations among participants. A
scanner or document stand includes a separate camera for
transmission of images of documents and objects and can be
zoomed and focused separately. These systems can have up to

three separate monitors for displaying persons, documents, and graphics simultaneously. Some single-monitor systems provide smaller windows in which images can be displayed separately.

Transmission between sites takes place over telephone, satellite, microwave, or cable networks. Such systems also provide diagnostic features to identify system failures that can be controlled from either facility. These videoconferencing systems may offer security features, including encryption with unique user-selectable keys for each transmission.

A number of vendors provide integrated multimedia conferencing facilities based on their proprietary codec devices. Until recently, these facilities could communicate only with other facilities using the same equipment. With the advent of compression standards and agreements on videoconferencing transmission standards, this drawback is being eliminated through the use of multiuser control units and carrier-operated multiprotocol videoconferencing services.

Personal Videoconferencing

Videoconferencing evolved from static boardrooms or conference room facilities, through rollabout systems and dedicated PCs, to PC add-ons and portable platforms. The rapid expansion of videoconferencing has been accomplished by a dramatic decline in price and improvement in performance.

In the 1980s videoconferencing facilities were dedicated conference rooms with studio settings costing hundreds of thousands of dollars. Technological progress made more compact rollabout systems possible, with prices ranging from $25,000 to $100,000. These have been supplemented and displaced by dedicated PC-based videoconferencing systems costing between $15,000 and $25,000 and add-on devices that turn an average desktop PC into a videoconferencing terminal for under $5,000. Portable videoconferencing platforms and personal hand-held communication devices will soon offer videoconferencing capabilities at a cost of about $1,000 per unit. Exhibit 7-4 illustrates these costs.

The most critical enabling technologies are compression algorithms and their implementation in codec designs. Originally based on expensive application-specific integrated circuits,

Exhibit 7-4. Costs of videoconferencing systems.

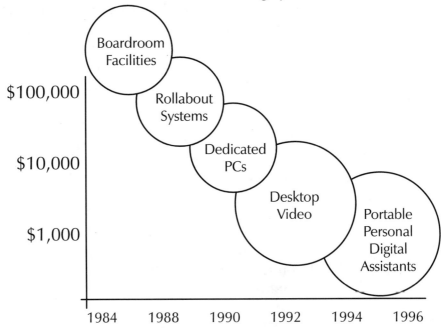

codecs are now based on more powerful general-purpose processors, making them cheaper and more flexible. Many semiconductor manufacturers make digital signal processors, which incorporate codec functions in a single microchip that can be embedded in the motherboard of an average PC. Semiconductor manufacturers see a large market for devices that provide all types of multimedia capabilities to computer platforms.

Widespread deployment of new video compression, audio compression, and international videoconferencing interoperability standards are also significant factors. Finally, progress in DSPs and microchip design is also responsible for the development of complex data transmission technologies. See Exhibit 7-5 for a summary of the enabling technologies.

Point-to-Point Videoconferencing

Most videoconferencing is basically point to point and is characterized by communications between two points, but it can involve more than two persons. Point-to-point videoconferencing categories include videotelephony, desktop-to-desktop,

Exhibit 7-5. Summary of enabling technologies.

Technology	Description of Impact on Videoconferencing
Compression	High-quality video is now possible at band-widths as low as 112 Kbps, which means lower transmission costs.
Codec design	Latest designs include general-purpose CPUs in codecs instead of more expensive applica-tion-speciÆc integrated circuits, making them cheaper and more Øexible.
Digital signal proces-sors (DSPs)	Various silicon chip development efforts are under way to enable codec functions at the microchip level.
Inverse multiplexors	This device can spread a high-speed data stream across multiple 56/64 Kbps circuits, allowing videoconferencing over lower-cost switched digital data services.
Multipoint control units (MCUs)	Complex hardware unit which allows the es-tablishment of multiprotocol videoconferenc-ing between dissimilar systems.
Interoperability stan-dards	These expand the utility of videoconferencing by facilitating communications between dis-similar systems.
H.320 compression standard	Widespread deployment of this video com-pression standard enables introduction of net-worked videoconferencing.
G.728 audio standard	Latest G.728 algorithm audio standard re-quires only 16 Kbps bandwidth, an improve-ment over G.711 and G.722 standards.
Isochronous networks	Special transmission technology facilitates vid-eoconferencing on existing LANs and WANs.
Desktop videoconferencing	Rapid development of low-cost videoconfer-encing alternatives using existing PC plat-forms.

(continued)

Exhibit 7-5. (continued)

Technology	Description of Impact on Videoconferencing
Video cameras	Video cameras can be more extensively controlled through the system, including manipulation at the other end.
Transmission facilities	Rapid growth in ISDN, ATM, and high-speed LANs and WANs provides more effective infrastructure.
Videoconferencing services	Major carriers are providing videoconferencing services with multiprotocol, multiuser capabilities.

and rollabout and boardroom conferencing. (Exhibit 7-6 compares these categories.)

Videotelephony

Videotelephony is consumer-level two-way video communications using existing telephone lines. It is strictly a person-to-person system with a small screen and low image frame rates. These systems are unsuitable for business, but their use by the general public promotes videoconferencing in all its forms throughout the economy.

Videotelephony was introduced as PicturePhone by AT&T in 1964 at the New York World's Fair. At the time, cost and operating problems did not make it viable. Japanese firms introduced a failed black-and-white still-images version in the mid-1980s. And AT&T introduced the first personal videotelephone, the VideoPhone 2500, in 1992.

Today a videophone is a telephone with a small video camera and screen based on compression microchip codecs. It connects through a standard telephone jack and provides a 3.3-inch color screen displaying video images at 2 to 10 fps, resulting in jerky and uneven images. The limited bandwidth of the telephone lines makes it hard to improve unless more powerful compression microchips are used. The videotelephone camera can focus up to nine feet from the console and accommodate several persons.

Exhibit 7-6. Point-to-point videoconferencing system.

Videophone	Consumer-level video product using standard telephone lines with relatively poor quality and small size video of 2 to 10 frames per second.
Desktop-to-desktop	Communication between PCs in two separate locations. Cameras may be optional, but voice teleconferencing and shared data, text, or images may be used.
Rollabout conferencing	Mobile videoconferencing system connecting through modems and digital lines with other rollabout or permanent videoconferencing facilities.
Boardroom conferencing	Involves studio-like special conference rooms equipped with videoconferencing transmission facilities. Requires higher-bandwidth transmission lines.

Desktop-to-Desktop Conferencing

Also known as point-to-point, desktop conferencing involves two users, or two small groups of viewers, gathered around a single PC screen. PCs communicate over special links or existing LANs and WANs with another suitably equipped PC. Video, voice, and data are transmitted and displayed in specific windows as if the participants were sitting face to face in a conference room or working side by side at a drawing board. These systems do not always include video cameras and often rely on voice interaction for continuity. Inflexion and tones communicated on a realtime basis are considered superior to voice mail or annotated e-mail transmissions.

Desktop-to-desktop sessions are also used to share drawings or plans and text or images of documents that all participants can see simultaneously. Systems may involve remote pointers, allowing participants to point out visual details for clarification and reference. Chalkboard or whiteboard facilities display simple drawings. Depending on input devices, images may be scanned from documents, bitmap files imported from databases, and independent notes made during the sessions. The latest products are being developed to use Internet and ordinary telephone lines but the quality of such transmissions is relatively poor.

Rollabout and Boardroom Videoconferencing

Rollabout and boardroom videoconferencing facilities are basically point-to-point systems, although increasingly these are being turned into multiuser conferencing systems through the use of multipoint control units. These systems are basically used by work groups to seek consensus on various policy or project issues and are arranged on a scheduled basis.

Multipoint Videoconferencing: The Ultimate Management Tool

A multipoint videoconferencing system involves three or more locations interacting simultaneously. The speaking location controls transmissions through voice activation or specific commands. Such conferencing systems also transmit multimedia data, including documents, images, drawings, and video clips. These transmissions can be acted on, annotated, and changed during the conference from any participating location.

Multipoint conferencing also provides connectivity with other sources of information from devices such as databases, fax machines, camcorders, digital cameras, scanners, or portable units in the field.

To implement conferencing beyond the two site configurations, an intelligent hub is needed at a central site to switch videoconferencing traffic between locations. Bandwidth capacity linking all the network sites must be sufficient to carry several multimedia traffic streams simultaneously. (Exhibit 7-7 illustrates the system).

Multipoint multimedia conferencing is implemented using a multipoint control unit (MCU) that performs the switching function in realtime, distributing correct audio and video signals to all participants. The MCUs are placed at any point in

Exhibit 7-7. Multipoint conferencing concepts.

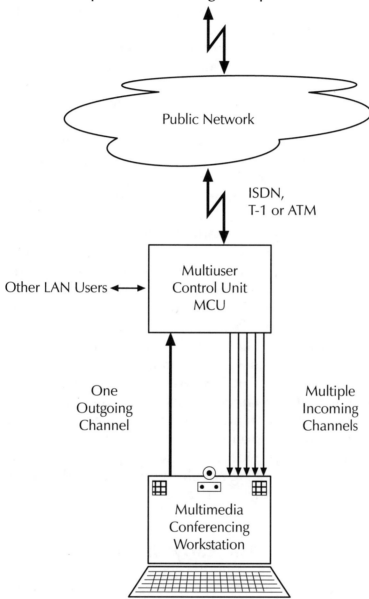

the videoconferencing network. They accept digitized signals from codecs and automatically route them to the proper sites.

MCUs were once proprietary products and operated only with codecs from a specific vendor. But Videoserver, Inc., of Lexington, Massachusetts, a start-up venture, revolutionized multipoint conferencing with its MCU unit compatible with codecs from a range of vendors. It meets the international multipoint videoconferencing standard H.243. Other videoconferencing equipment vendors have developed MCU equipment to accept signals from codecs other than their own units. These MCUs represent complex and precise technology with powerful processors and extensive microprocessor-based software systems. Typically they can handle eight to sixteen locations, at prices ranging from $10,000 to $25,000 per port. MCUs can also be leased from major carriers, such as AT&T, Sprint, and MCI Communications, to act as bridging facilities between videoconferencing systems of various vendors.

Geography and timing are important when evaluating multiuser conferencing. If conferencing sites are relatively close, an MCU might be worth buying to implement a private videoconferencing network. If users are widely distributed or mobile, carrier multiuser videoconferencing services are more cost-effective. Ownership of MCUs ensures complete control over scheduling of multimedia conferences and guarantees the most efficient bandwidth. Reliance on carrier services may require advance scheduling and does not always guarantee that all interactive features will be operational.

The introduction of low-cost desktop videoconferencing, multipoint control technology, and high-bandwidth networks, as well as videoconferencing services by major carriers, is paving the way toward group videoconferencing. Groupware software and desktop videoconferencing products are making group videoconferencing possible without requiring individual employees to leave their work areas.

The Early Users

Various types of organizations were early users of videoconferencing:

■ *Large corporations.* Installation and communications costs limited usage to high-level corporate board meetings, executive briefings, and financial and promotional applications. Because of involvement with information technology, MIS organizations of large corporations were also early adopters of videoconferencing, particularly of the lower-cost rollabout systems for management development and executive development functions.

- *Financial environment.* Finance videoconferencing has made inroads in mergers and acquisitions, financial reviews of corporate performance, portfolio management, and loans approvals. Some financial institutions are now considering nationwide multimedia conferencing systems to provide video images of their executives to all customers.

- *Health care organizations.* Remote diagnosis and medical consultation are the most significant applications. Videoconferencing is of significant value in remote and rural areas where major hospitals and small local clinics may be separated by hundreds of miles.

- *Project management.* Early adopters were found in engineering design and project coordination functions. Technology companies involved in complex projects, such as design or integrated circuits, aircraft, electronic systems, or processing plants, require continual information sharing and technical support. Multimedia conferencing is very cost-effective and is a major factor leading to the development of concurrent or simultaneous engineering activities.

- *Human resources.* Videoconferencing is used in interviewing, recruiting, training new employees, and evaluating others for transfer. Among major recruitment organizations, Management Recruiters International of Cleveland has deployed hundreds of desktop videoconferencing units throughout its worldwide offices. Corporate training and just-in-time factory training are also early users of videoconferencing and interactive multimedia training systems.

- *Sales and marketing.* These uses are evident in the deployment of interactive multimedia kiosks, customer support for complex projects, and communications with original equipment manufacturer clients by technology equipment manufacturers.

- *Judiciary.* Legal depositions and prisoner arraignments can be accomplished without the necessity of personal appearances. The O. J. Simpson trial was a well-known case of courtroom multimedia applications.

▪ *Law enforcement.* One of the most desirable multimedia applications being studied by law enforcement officials, a system to identify images of terrorist and wanted criminal suspects, involves infrared cameras that record human traffic flow in airports, for example, and develop digitized images. Digital inputs could be linked instantly with databases storing infrared images, leading to immediate identification and apprehension. This application relies on the concept of a distinctive infrared aura given off by every individual.

Digital cameras, key in law enforcement multimedia systems, may become standard evidence-gathering tools at crime scenes. They could identify doctored drivers licenses.

Facial recognition systems are among the most promising law enforcement applications. The Applied Research Projects Agency (ARPA) of the Department of Defense for years has funded research into pattern recognition technologies using neural networks and artificial intelligence. Now these technologies are being transferred into the civilian sectors.

▪ *TV broadcasting.* Interviews can be conducted in remote locations, often on a multipoint basis.

▪ *Security industry.* Videoconferencing can be used for remote monitoring and surveillance purposes.

Exhibit 7-8 shows the major uses of videoconferencing.

Videoconferencing Services for All

By the end of 1993 20,000 videoconferencing systems using private communication links had been installed in the United States. Some operated by long-distance telephone carriers and business enterprises specializing in videoconferencing services to business and the general public.

Such services will proliferate and become as common as fax machines. Within a year or two videoconferencing systems will cost less than $1,000 per unit and will become an option for PCs like modems or multimedia capabilities today. Some products are already cheaper than that, but the quality of images is still poor, and they are not yet suitable for business use.

Exhibit 7-8. Major uses of videoconferencing.

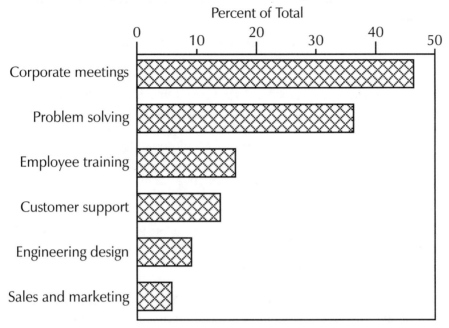

Competitive factors such as standards of data transmission, declining DSP prices, and the introduction of more powerful PCs and workstations, have begun to eliminate the need for special videoconferencing equipment and the dominance by specialized vendors such as Compression Labs, PictureTel, VTEL, and others that provide systems based on proprietary codecs incompatible with any other system. Established videoconferencing suppliers are coming out with lower-cost alternatives as well as MCUs that allow multiuser videoconferencing between systems with different protocols.

Several product groups can be identified in the videoconferencing market. Established suppliers are active in several market segments—videophones, desktop videoconferencing systems, rollabout products, and custom-built boardroom videoconferencing centers. There are also videoconferencing services supplied by major long-distance carriers, as well as specialized service organizations and brokers. Exhibit 7-9 identifies these market segments and the major vendors active in each market.

At the forefront of the desktop videoconferencing revo-

Exhibit 7-9. Multimedia conferencing vendors.

Product Category	Major Vendors in This Market
Videophones	AT&T, BT North America, Hitachi America
Desktop video-conferencing	AT&T, Compaq Computer, Compression Labs, Dolch Computer Systems, Extron Electronics, Extel Communications, Fujitsu Industry Networks, Future Labs, IBM, InSoft, Intel, InVision Systems, Microsoft, Novell Multimedia, Northern Telecom, PictureTel, Radish Communications, Sharevision Technology (Creative Technology), Sony, Target Technologies, VideoLabs, VTEL
LAN-based videoconferencing	Datapoint, DEC, Hewlett-Packard, Intel, Intervision, Microsoft, Silicon Graphics, Starlight Networks, Sun Solutions
Rollabout videoconferencing	BT North America, Compression Labs, GPT Video Systems, Hitachi America, Mitsubishi Electronics America, NEC America, Panasonic Broadcast & TV Systems, PictureTel, Videoconferencing Systems, VTEL
Boardroom videoconferencing	Compression Labs, GPT Video Systems, Mitsubishi Electronics America, Picturetel, VTEL
Videoconferencing services	AT&T Global Business Video Services Group, Affinity Communications, Ascom Timeplex, Bell Atlantic, Connexus, MCI Communications, SP Telecom, Sprint Video

lution are: Apple, Alpha Systems Labs, AT&T, Avistar, Compression Labs, Comtech Labs, Datapoint, Fujitsu Networks, FutureTel, IBM, InSoft, InVision Systems, KLT Telecom, Northern Telecom, Nuts Technologies, Paradise Software, Peregrine Systems, PictureTel, Target Technologies, Unisys, Video Conference Communications, ViewPoint Systems, VIVO Software, and VTEL.

8

The New Training Imperative

Corporate training, the major multimedia application, is expanding as multimedia-capable PCs proliferate and effective multimedia development tools are created. The trend toward the interactive enterprise and the virtual corporation, requiring specific skills on short notice, creates a powerful training incentive. Managers intent on moving into an intensely competitive future must have the necessary resources to assemble and train work groups rapidly.

The most common training comes in CD-ROM form, which is relatively cheap to produce and distribute. CD-recordable drives make it possible to produce and replicate an in-house training program with great speed. Training titles are available in just about every industry. Because keeping up-to-date on training is important, some organizations are building CD-ROM LANs to store a variety of interactive multimedia training programs. Most computer-based-training (CBT) applications in the corporate world are being networked for more effective delivery.

For years large corporations with considerable budgets and patience have been implementing CBT. Today's technologies make it comparable to conventional training, but with these added benefits: self-paced instruction, shorter learning times, precise performance measurements, and lower costs per worker. It also offers just-in-time training, so critical for interactive enterprises.

A Business Research Group survey shows that 69 percent of respondents believe corporate training is the most common and valuable multimedia application with the greatest return on investment potential. The National Education and Training Group's survey of 512 companies shows that over 60 percent of respondents plan to increase their use of interactive multimedia training within a year, while only 18 percent intend to increase conventional classroom training.

CBT still has a long way to go. U.S. companies spend $43 million annually on training, and interactive multimedia training is only a small percentage of that budget. On the other hand, a Frost & Sullivan study suggests that one in three multimedia application sales is made for training purposes.

Another assessment comes from a Dataquest survey of information services managers and directors about training budgets and CBT attitudes. According to that survey, technology-based training, including CBT, is represented by 20 percent of all information technology training and education budgeting; 74 percent of executives who responded are implementing CBT, and 45 percent use interactive multimedia CBT applications.

Training Development Tools

The bulk of effort in developing courseware lies in extracting existing knowledge from the workers and experts involved.

> Critical step: Performance measurements and remedial routines must be designed by training and psychology experts for the courseware to provide adequate assessments of workers, their ability to absorb the training, and their potential to become effective in the new tasks facing them.

Most often, applications are developed by a team, with information from subject experts, educational psychologists, and designers. Advanced authoring systems make it relatively easy to design and deploy interactive multimedia courseware without extensive programming and computer skills, but there is nevertheless a significant effort required in conceptualization and audience needs analysis before a successful training program can be developed.

Training Program Economics and Benefits

Multimedia training programs have high development costs and take a long time to develop—up to eighty to two hundred hours to produce just one hour of final training courseware. Only companies with large numbers of workers to be trained can justify the expense of in-house courseware development. Then they can spend over $50,000 annually to produce, update, and maintain a single CBT course. In short, CBT is expensive to develop; it is cost-effective to distribute and maintain only when more than two hundred workers from several locations are trained.

Professional trainers and educators view interactive multimedia training as a natural way to learn because it provides the user with an experience involving sight, sound, and interaction. User involvement improves absorption and retention rate. Generally published statistics from the training community show that students retain 20% of what they hear; 50% of what they see and hear simultaneously, and 90% of what they see, hear, and do. In traditional training, a single instructor does not have time to ensure the full participation of each student and evaluate whether he or she has fully grasped the information.

Controlled studies of multimedia training applications claim extraordinary learning efficiencies. Learning times for professionals have decreased 30 to 35 percent, and competence levels have improved by about 20 percent compared with traditional methods.

CBT training, an extension of the best live training sessions and instructors available, provides training at the convenience of users, reduces travel time and cost, and reduces the number of trainers. And no matter how long it takes trainees to absorb the knowledge, the system remains in place. It can be replayed precisely as often as needed. At the same time, it administers tests and quizzes to measure performance and the need for training program adjustments, and it produces management reports on group performances.

When training costs are analyzed on a life cycle basis—including continuous costs of delivery, such as participants' time, travel expenses, housing costs, instructor costs and expenses, training materials, and equipment—CBT costs will be *two to three times less* than conventional training. CBT decentralization of training delivery reduces the expenses of participation in the long run.

Popular Multimedia Training Categories

Management development and supervisory skills are the most common training course categories, followed by technical skills and knowledge training programs. Communications skills, basic computer skills, new methods and procedures, and customer relations are also popular training programs. Others include clerical and secretarial skills, personal growth, executive development, labor relations, wellness, sales skills, customer service, and remedial basic education.

General Categories

Multimedia courses fall into five major categories:

1. *Employee relations.* These courses focus on oral communications, leadership, team building, performance appraisal, goal setting, hiring and selection criteria, delegation skills, motivation, listening skills, time management, interpersonal diplomacy, outplacement, retirement issues, face-to-face problem solving, and employee theft and fraud, among others.
2. *Decision making.* The focus is on development of personal characteristics conducive to management—for example, training in management of change, decisiveness, strategic planning, written communications, negotiating skills, stress management, public speaking, and conduct of meetings.
3. *Finance.* This area deals with budgeting, project time and cost controls, risk analysis, loss prevention, and generally managing profit-and-loss business units.
4. *Marketing.* This growing area deals with market intelligence, sales training, sales motivation, selling skills, customer services, and telemarketing.

5. *Regulation compliance.* Another growing area, it prepares management for handling issues of safety, security, environmental controls, labor unions, and other regulatory questions pertaining to the business of the corporation and enforced by local or national authorities.

Industrial Training Programs

These programs fall under five general categories:

1. *Fundamentals.* These courses focus on basic theory and testing on algebra, decimals, numbers, mathematics, Ohm's law, reading skills, statistics, AC/DC basics, electronic circuits, fractions, digital electronics, microprocessors, measuring, and similar topics.
2. *Specific equipment and processes.* These courses deal with manufacturing processes and equipment—for example, papermaking, pipefitting, scaffolding, lubrication, process controls, composite materials, hand tools, pneumatics, gauging practices, robotics, programming, ladder diagrams, precision instruments, semiconductors, industrial controls, and switches.
3. *Maintenance.* This particularly fertile field for multimedia applications trains workers in the maintenance of complex equipment and machinery. Applications include troubleshooting pumps, compressors, turbines, DC motors, and electrical and electronic circuits.
4. *Safety.* These programs may include training in the use of masks, purification of contaminated atmospheres, asbestos handling, transport of hazardous materials and chemicals, nuclear materials handling, and toxic chemicals storage. Operation of trucks, trains, forklifts, and other industrial vehicles and materials-handling equipment also falls under this category, as do evacuation procedures and securing the welfare of industrial personnel.
5. *Just-in-time (JIT) training.* This category is designed to assist workers experiencing difficulty with machine tools or assembly line components. JIT training system ques-

tions the worker, collects responses, and determines the solution. It provides specific knowledge explaining the situation and demonstrating a procedure to fix the problem or get the system going again. It focuses on the training function to minimize similar stoppage in the future.

Health Care Training

Medical and health care training applications target physicians, nurses, paramedics, drug representatives, and other health care workers. It is particularly useful in an area entailing demonstrations of complex procedures and explanations of physiological mechanisms involved in drug therapies. For example, training courses in this sector include such topics as AIDS, anatomy of the heart, intravenous therapies and procedures, coronary disease, emergency protocols, health hazards in the workplace, infection control, human genetics, renal analysis, and sexually transmitted diseases.

Special Training Opportunities

Information Technology

A large number of training courses explain the use of complex hardware and software systems. Courses deal with computers in general, customer information control system concepts and facilities, mass storage systems, printing systems, data communications, networking, software engineering, and UNIX, SQL, and C programming. New initiatives from software vendors also exist. Lotus is developing Multimedia Smart-Help CD-ROM-based help using animation and sound designed to assist end users in using 1-2-3 Windows and Notes products.

> The trend: CD-ROM disks containing the
> software and training and help.

Government Agencies

Local, state, and federal agencies use multimedia training to explain bureaucratic activities and law enforcement procedures. The training system applications range from environmental controls, rules, and regulations to specialized law enforcement, driver training for police officers and state troopers, and safe driving and arrest procedures. The CIA uses simulators to update its field agents at embassies throughout the world. Multimedia CBT courseware is being used by police departments and law enforcement academies to cover topics such as street behavior of police officers, crisis intervention, interrogation, forensic science, and corrections. The National Aeronautics and Space Administration was an early user of multimedia training for new personnel and space shuttle subsystems familiarization.

Military Services

Among the largest spenders on multimedia CBT systems, the army, navy, and air force are all involved in training and were among the early adopters of the technology. The navy uses multimedia training at its guided missile cruiser and destroyer education center for weapons operations and systems maintenance. Similar systems handle basic operator and maintenance training at the fleet antisubmarine warfare training center. Multimedia systems have been developed for training in turret and gunnery procedures of army battle tanks and maintenance of helicopters. The Army National Guard has used multimedia for armored platoon leadership training programs.

Multimedia Training Users: Cases in Point

American Airlines

One of the largest users of multimedia training systems, this corporation pioneered the use of multimedia for flight crew training. Its pilot training center in Dallas uses interactive multimedia to cut down on the use of expensive full-scale flight simulators. The company spent about $350,000 for a pilot training system for the MD-11 aircraft and expects to expand multimedia training to other aircraft. By enhancing its Sabre Assisted Instruction system with 152 hours of multimedia courseware,

American trained 60 percent of its 80,000 employees in international security, cargo handling, ticketing, and passenger handling.

Bethlehem Steel

A heavy user of interactive videodisk systems since 1985, Bethlehem Steel uses a system based in Intel's DVI technology designed to teach employees how to analyze sales statistics, inventory, and production to control precisely the availability of specific types of steel. It is an early example of multimedia training in support of simultaneous engineering activities in which automotive companies and their suppliers collaborate closely in the manufacture of products to respond precisely to the market. The courses, given to over 5,000 employees, reduced training time by 20 to 40 percent. Retention rates increased by a similar percentage range.

> Key to success: Training is available on demand at any time of day or night.

Federal Express

Federal Express's interactive multimedia driver safety training system in the interactive videodisk category primarily addresses attitudinal aspects of driving and promotes awareness of road hazards. Other organizations using similar applications are Shell International, Pacific Bell, and police forces throughout the country. Federal Express uses animated CBT programs to train customers on how to ship packages and train employees in new technologies.

IBM

IBM is a heavy user of multimedia training in marketing and on the factory floor. Workstations at the Poughkeepsie, New York, assembly plant provide step-by-step guidance to factory workers explaining details of differing processes. As a result IBM claims $800,000 in annual savings. The company also uses the Simulator System Training device from Performax, which

includes video camera, microphones, and videotape and provides automated sales skills training through role playing. Employees' reactions are recorded for review and evaluation.

Northern Telecom

This large telecommunications company reduced its training
time for switch maintenance training programs using CBT. This
approach reduced the time it takes to train customers by 25
percent, provided consistent high performance, and increased
scheduling flexibility. The courseware consists of eighty hours
of instruction and eighty hours of hands-on training and is distributed to customers on a hard disk drive card. Other companies are developing a means for delivering such multimedia
training courseware via satellite TV systems.

Sears Roebuck

Facing a very high turnover rate and continual need to train
salespeople on twenty-six major merchandise lines, Sears developed a Brand Central education network as a solution. Involving 800 PCs using multimedia software and hardware in
all stores' associates training rooms, it was accessible to all employees at any time. Salespeople needing updates on product
lines under their responsibility can turn to these multimedia
systems. The system administers objective comprehension tests
and allows precise measurements of each employee's degree of
learning.

Union Pacific

This application acts as a catalyst to overhaul the entire corporate culture. To make the railroad more competitive, a sophisticated network, permitting conductors to send and receive
information about activities on a realtime basis, was installed
on the trains. Unusual methods were employed to train conductors, accountants, and other personnel on how to communicate with each other all the way down the line. An interactive
multimedia training system was developed using QUEST authoring software and deployed at seventeen training sites in

crew rooms and rail yards throughout the western United States.

U.S. Air Force

The self-paced multimedia training for fighter pilots and weapons systems operators covers instrument orientation, radar operations, aerial navigation, infrared theory, and electronic warfare for a number of aircraft.

Spotlight on the Future

Intensifying global competition, more demanding customers, and shorter product life cycles will influence the future types and quantity of formal corporate training. Multimedia CBT solutions are expected to play an increasing role in this process.

There is already a shift in the corporate perception of future training challenges. In order of priority, these are new market strategies, organizational missions, concurrent engineering, technological change, product quality enhancement, customer services, corporate culture, project team staffing, and productivity improvement. Other issues are centralization and decentralization, mergers and acquisitions, succession planning, remedial and basic education, and international competitive intelligence. Not all are ideal targets for multimedia training applications, but there is little doubt that as multimedia platforms and personal videoconferencing capabilities proliferate, most training programs will turn to multimedia technologies.

9

Competitive Marketing With Multimedia

Marketing—the least automated business function—can benefit from the introduction of competitive methods that are now available at acceptable costs.

Boosting Promotion Programs With Multimedia

Complex products and services that require customization can be better promoted with interactive multimedia—for example, financial products and services, travel itineraries, drug application therapies, real estate promotions, computer software systems, complex equipment installations, and architectural and engineering projects. Sales applications are becoming popular too as marketing organizations and advertising agencies introduce more automation into the sales and marketing functions. One difficulty in this area is that many small advertising agencies are not yet knowledgeable enough to implement interactive marketing programs for clients. Some large agencies are exploring the use of interactive marketing, and many have designed electronic brochures, CD-ROMs, merchandising kiosks, and virtual reality simulations. In most cases, however, the projects were developed with the assistance of specialized multimedia content and application developers.

Multimedia applications can take a number of forms—for example:

- *Automated catalogs:*
  Interactive CD-ROM-based software listing numerous products with images and videos and data.
- *Electronic brochures:*
  Typically an interactive diskette with images and data about a particular product mailed to prospects.
- *Multimedia kiosks:*
  Interactive multimedia systems matching customers with a specific product or service; may be unattended or operated by sales personnel.
- *Information booths:*
  Stand-alone interactive systems designed to guide customers to specific product sale locations.
- *Travel advisers:*
  Provides videos, images, maps, and data of destinations for travel agencies.
- *Ticket dispensers:*
  Interactive systems using audio and video to sell tickets or issue coupons for specific product discounts.
- *Rental agents:*
  Interactive systems offering selections of rentals, such as automobiles and contract transactions.
- *Real estate:*
  Video and walk-through systems describing residential or commercial properties, with full financial details.
- *Yellow Pages:*
  Interactive TV form of advertising with images of products and services and automatic reservations.
- *Pharmaceuticals:*
  Interactive explanations of new drugs and therapies for physicians and hospitals.
- *Virtual mall:*
  Virtual reality simulation of a shopping mall with capabilities to order products displayed.
- *Mobile sales:*
  Interactive multimedia presentations based on portable and notebook computer platforms.

Interactivity: An Attention Getter

Interactivity dramatically alters conventional transactions among sellers, buyers, promoters, advertising agencies, and the media. It captures and holds end users' attention through user involvement in the process. The consumer selects information and decides on a purchase without help or prompting from a sales associate.

Interactive marketing can target individuals better than traditional TV or direct mail can, and it can provide a precise record of tastes, interests, preferences, and purchase history. It establishes customer relationships and permits the development of products to satisfy demands based on personal demographics or timing. Exhibit 9-1 compares interactive marketing with traditional methods.

Interactivity reaches customers or prospects and keeps their attention longer than a TV spot or newspaper or magazine ad can. Prospective automobile buyers, for example, select a model and then compare colors, interiors, engine sizes, options, and payment plans. This type of attention is far too costly for an actual salesperson to provide.

> Added beneÆt: Consistency of information even when delivered in various sequence formats to different prospects.

Interaction can mean new marketing industry challenges. It produces large quantities of detailed buyer profiles; means re-

Exhibit 9-1. Interactive and traditional marketing compared.

	Interactive Marketing	Mass Media Marketing	Direct Mail Marketing
Target audience	Individuals	Populations	Product focus
Delivery method	Interactive TV, on-line services, PCs	TV, magazines, newspapers	Mailing Lists
End user	Active	Passive	Passive
Products	Financial services Fashion clothes Travel Real estate Automobiles Software	Consumer goods Foods Beer Automobiles	Travel Credit cards Publications Books Automobiles Clothes

engineering interaction among suppliers, producers, and consumers; and as a result creates resistance in established marketing circles. But as interactive marketing becomes more common, consumers will look at interactive TV and their PCs as the most convenient sources of product information on demand and be more likely to make their purchases from companies providing information in a timely and entertaining manner.

Multimedia in Advertising

As multimedia authoring and video editing software increasingly is used for the production of TV spots, commercial online projects, TV pilots, CD-ROM promotions, diskettes, merchandising kiosks, Internet selling, electronic retailing services, and virtual reality simulations, agencies are creating special groups or departments dedicated to interactive advertising and entering into strategic ventures with specialized software and content development firms. This activity is confined to large worldwide agencies with the resources to investigate interactive marketing concepts and implications. Exhibit 9-2 lists some of the activities of these major advertising agencies. Smaller agencies are not likely to get involved in multimedia unless it is funded by a client. It is not surprising, then, that corporate marketing departments often undertake multimedia projects on their own.

Advertising Production

Traditionally, advertising agencies create a TV spot using a storyboard and an outside production house to shoot and assemble the video footage. Changes require repeating the process (storyboard, reshooting, and presentations) until the client is satisfied, but this process can deplete a budget. Using off-the-shelf video editing software and a PC, agencies can accelerate the production process and save money.

Production house charges range up to $1,000 an hour, but with PC-based video editing, an agency can do comparable work at a fraction of the cost. Development tools like Adobe

Exhibit 9-2. Interactive advertising activities of major agencies.

Advertising Agency	Involvement in Interactive Marketing Projects
BBDO Worldwide	Interactive task force since 1992 Involved with interactive network Testing interactive commercials for Chrysler
Bates USA	Dedicated task group since June 1992 Study on potential for interactive media marketing With IT Network testing interactive TV in Dallas and Denver
Bozell, Jacobs, Kenyon & Eckhardt	BJK&E interactive group since 1994 Developing interactive CD-ROM and CD-I products Involved with Full Service Network interactive TV pilot project Plans to offer interactive marketing capabilities to other agencies
Chiat/Day	Task force on interactive media Creating online advertising for Coca-Cola Minority interest in Interactive Connection, an on-line service start-up
D'Arcy Masius Benton & Bowles	Informal interactive task force Projects for Citicorp, Cannon, and BellSouth Intends to create content for interactive TV pilots Acquired a multimedia agency
DDB Needham	Interactive marketing research program for subscribers at $25,000 annually Developing content materials for multimedia merchandising kiosks for Wal-Mart, K-Mart, and Nobody Beats the Wiz
Foote, Cone & Belding Communications	Electronic media task force since 1990 Partnership with IT Network for interactive TV projects Developed CD-ROM and kiosk projects for Mazda Motors

(continued)

Exhibit 9-2. (continued)

Advertising Agency	Involvement in Interactive Marketing Projects
Grey Advertising	Gray interactive internal task force Assisting start-up Mosaic Communications to develop Internet advertising Involved with interactive TV pilot project FSN in Orlando, Florida
J. Walter Thomson	JWT/On-Line since 1990 Testing interactive advertising in 30,000 households with cable TV company Created interactive advertising for Ford, Citibank, and Kodak on Prodigy and Compuserve networks Participate in several interactive TV projects in the United States and Canada
Ketchum Communications	Interactive group since 1992 Explores interactive marketing in advertising, PR, direct mail, and Yellow Pages Developed CD-ROMs and kiosk projects for Acura Concerned about interactive TV
Leo Burnett Company	Interactive Marketing Group Developed interactive advertising for Oldsmobile and MacDonald's Active with Prodigy, NBC, and America Online
Lintas Worldwide	Several interactive TV pilots, including FSN Created online system for Chevrolet headquarters and sales operations Special network for GM Parts Division linking 3,500 engineers
McCann-Erickson Worldwide	Created McCann Interactive to promote new media within the group Early sponsor of Media Labs at MI Projects for GM, Johnson & Johnson, Coca-Cola, Nestlé, and others Interactive TV test in Springfeld, Massachusetts, in 1990 with AT&T, GM, and Coca-Cola

NW Ayer	Developed interactive advertising using Prodigy and Newsweek InterActive
	Interactive TV schemes in Seattle, Denver, and Mount Prospect, Illinois
	Educates ``creatives" how interactivity works
	Alliance with Interactive Marketing Technologies, King of Prussia, Pennsylvania
Ogilvy & Mather Direct	Interactive marketing group since 1983
	Undisputed interactive advertising leader among advertising agencies
	Early participant in the videotext project for Kraft
	Currently involved with every interactive platform
Saatchi & Saatchi	Interactive Plus, a dedicated group originally supporting cable TV advertising
	Developing a study of future interactive TV pilot participants
	Working with Sony Imagesoft on several video game projects
Young & Rubicam	Researching all interactive platforms for clients
	Involved with FSN pilot for U.S. Postal Service and Holiday Inn
	Toronto ofÆce active with Videoway pilot in Quebec on behalf of Ford

Premiere and Photoshop, Elastic Reality, and Macromedia Director provide full-motion, full-screen playback and fancy special effects like morphing for manipulation of rough commercials until everyone is satisfied and then transfer to a tape for TV broadcasting. So far, only a few of the largest agencies (BBDO, Foote, Cone & Belding, and Ogilvy & Mather) have taken advantage of these tools.

Interactive Multimedia Advertising

Interactive multimedia advertising originated with the electronic brochure. Now interactive messages are also available on CD-ROM disks, targeting multimedia PC platforms and CD-ROM players. More sophisticated interactive advertising takes the form of networked kiosks or displays that present information intermixed with advertising messages for products and local services.

More sophisticated systems provide messages to professional target audiences. Physician Computer Network in Laurence Harbor, New Jersey, provides free PCs to physicians in return for a commitment to review up to thirty-two advertising messages every month and answer clinically oriented questions interactively. These inputs are combined into statistics sold to pharmaceutical manufacturers and market research organizations.

Interactive TV Advertising

Agencies are now involved with interactive TV pilot programs being run by regional Bell telephone companies and some cable TV operations. Pilots involve the wiring of hundreds and thousands of households to observe viewing patterns and viewers' reactions to interactive advertising and other services. In some cases, these services are also extended to local schools, libraries, and businesses. Future Vision of America, West Conshohocken, Pennsylvania, in a pioneering venture, is developing interactive advertising programs that allow companies with PCs and modems to send interactive messages to targeted homes for under $100 per month. Advertisers can insert interactive spots or overlays to add response elements to the display on an individual address basis. Contests, special promotions, and discounts are an important feature of these services, and viewers also have a means of storing selected commercials for future review.

Research is determining the motivation that will make the viewer want to interact. Advertisers are searching for methods to minimize viewer inactivity—equivalent to viewers' zapping commercials on conventional TV.

Virtual Reality in Advertising

The most sophisticated interactive advertising is **virtual reality** (VR) simulation, which is usually presented in a special form related to the product or service. VR, touted as the ultimate user interface, simulates an environment through immersive or interactive means. The immersive approach requires 3-D display devices such as goggles or head-mounted displays worn by the user, who then sees a virtual world change as he or she moves. User movements are relayed through a tracking system to a database of objects representing the simulated 3-D environment that the viewer visualizes. VR systems are expensive, however, and they require considerable computer skills and powerful workstations to render complex graphics in realtime. Exhibit 9-3 illustrates the principle of a VR simulation.

Horizon Entertainment in St. Louis created Virtual Voyage, a 2^1/$_2$-minute VR experience promoting Cutty Sark whisky for Hiram Walker & Sons. In this promotion, consumers in bars, restaurants, and other locations have an opportunity to "sail" a ship on rough seas smuggling liquor during Prohibition while being intercepted by hostile biplanes from above. The system uses a 360° HMD (a head-mounted display looking like a helmet) and a $200,000 high-performance Silicon Graphics workstation. It cost $1 million to develop.

Electronic Brochures and Catalogs

Electronic brochures and catalogs are the first and simplest examples of interactive multimedia marketing products. Exhibit 9-4 compares the main characteristics of the two categories.

Electronic Brochures

Electronic brochures, interactive alternatives for direct mail brochures targeted at special user groups, consist of a magnetic diskette with an interactive program that includes images, graphics, animation, sound, text, and data. Because of diskette storage limitations, video is seldom used, but very brief clips are possible using compression.

Electronic brochures are more effective than conventional multicolor direct mail brochures. Their interactivity gives the appearance of message customization, and instant feedback provides personalized calculations of benefits or investment returns. There is also the additional impact of animation and sound effects.

Electronic brochures produce responses of up to 12 per-

Exhibit 9-3. Virtual reality basics.

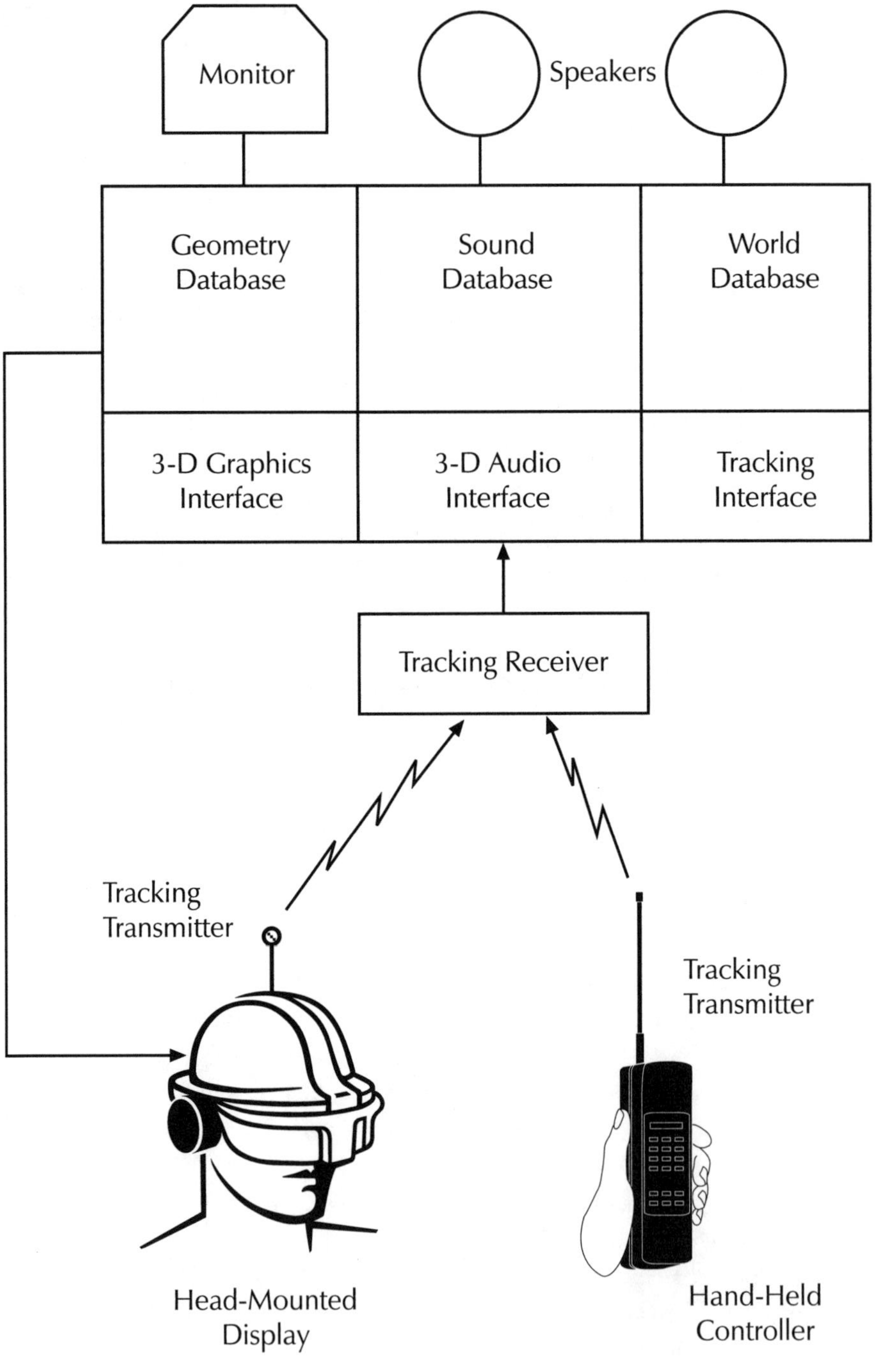

Monitor

Speakers

Geometry Database	Sound Database	World Database
3-D Graphics Interface	3-D Audio Interface	Tracking Interface

Tracking Receiver

Tracking Transmitter

Tracking Transmitter

Head-Mounted Display

Hand-Held Controller

Exhibit 9-4. Electronic brochure and catalog characteristics.

Electronic Brochure	Electronic Catalog
Single-product presentation	Multiple-product presentations
Targets individual consumers	and lists
with PCs	CD-ROM-based product
Generates and qualiÆes leads	Industrial and commercial use
High response rate due to inter-	Directory type of applications
activity	Requires multimedia PC plat-
Competitive with direct mail	form
Interactive diskette product	Runs on other CD-ROM
Standard PC platforms	players
Graphics, animation, and audio	Video, audio, animation, and
Limited video	graphics
Relatively low cost of produc-	Networking options
tion (Æve cents to two dollars	Order placement capabilities
for diskette)	Higher cost of production (one
	to two dollars per CD disk)

cent—higher than conventional direct mail, where a 1 percent response is the norm. Electronic brochures are used to generate or qualify sales leads or answer standard questions without a sales call that can run as high as $400.

The development costs can range from $10,000 to $500,000, with an average of between $20,000 and $30,000 for a simple program. The cost of diskettes depends on the number of copies produced and mailed; the range is five cents to two dollars per unit.

GM Buick was a pioneer user. In 1986 it promoted its new models to PC users using animation, color options, and competitive information. As an incentive to view, it contained a simulated golf game for user entertainment. Ford and Chrysler were also early users. Among other companies using electronic brochures are AIG, AT&T, Bristol-Myers-Squibb, Citibank, Compaq, Dun & Bradstreet, IBM, Intel, Merck Sharpe & Dohme, Mitsubishi, New York Power Authority, Netherlands Foreign Investment Agency, NYNEX, Prodigy, the U.S. Army, Upjohn, *USA Today*, Western Union, and Zenith Data Systems.

Electronic Catalogs

The catalog is an extension of the electronic brochure. It is designed to promote products among industrial distributors and may include automatic ordering features. Interactive multimedia presentations replace conventional paper catalogs and brochures and allow the industrial buyer to select products and make competitive comparisons. The catalogs are based on CD-ROMs and require a multimedia PC platform to use. Some electronic catalogs include an ordering system and can be used to place direct orders to the distributor in a networked environment for immediate processing.

The cost of producing and mailing a CD-ROM-based catalog is about $1.30 per disk in large quantities, which compares favorably with the cost of printing and distributing a typical eighty-page merchandising catalog. At a relatively low cost, therefore, electronic catalogs offer strong impact, instant ordering facilities, and quick updating.

Typical users are organizations whose images of constantly changing fashions and products are important—for example, Sears and Nordstrom. CD-ROMs are used in other industries where images and videos illustrating the use of products is important to the selling process.

Product Merchandising Systems

Designed to assist sales personnel in specialty stores in selecting the best possible product or service for their customers, **product systems** are PC based and are operated by store sales personnel. These are multimedia presentation programs with direct interaction for ordering specific products. Sales are not made automatically through the system; rather, content materials are designed to involve the customer and salesperson simultaneously. Typical sites for product merchandising systems are furniture stores, hardware chains, auto showrooms, beauty salons, and home improvement centers. Once in operation, these systems capture market and demographic data.

These systems are most useful for complex products or products requiring customization. (Some examples are listed in Exhibit 9-5.) Customer requirements are matched against a database of product information supported by images, animation, and videos. Earlier systems using mostly text and data

Exhibit 9-5. Typical multimedia product merchandising systems.

Company	System Characteristics and Capabilities
DesignCenter Weyerhauser Subsidiary	Creates designs of certain home improvements and provides bill of materials and pricing Installed in over 100 home centers and hardware stores Credited with $250 million worth of designs during first year of operation Stores claim tripling of closing rates for these products
Florsheim Shoes	Touch-screen-controlled system displaying images of over 300 styles of shoes with available colors and sizes Keeps inventory of specific styles and sizes and informs salespeople where they are available Includes transaction processing on input of client data and credit card number
Mannington Resilient Floors	Dealer-operated touch screen interface displays floor covering patterns and colors based on customer room layout and size inputs Tracks who looks at which pattern and colors and includes sales training module
Rover Group	Provides a network of 750 dealers a system for customizing Rover vehicles in showrooms Customer indicates options wanted and in seconds system develops an image of what the vehicle looks like Also checks Rover vehicle database at all dealerships and corporate mainframe for earliest availability
Steelcase	Sales improvement system assists sales personnel in selling office furniture System displays video alternatives based on customer image, performance requirements, and financial standing Computes benefits and competitive assessments

were highly interactive but not as effective as the current systems, which incorporate multimedia content.

Merchandising Kiosks

The most popular form of interactive multimedia merchandising is the stand-alone unattended kiosk. It can provide information only or perform purchasing transactions. A typical system consists of a touch screen, a computer, a CD-ROM or videodisk, speakers, printers, and credit card readers, all combined in an attractive enclosure. Keyboards are used in some systems for entering names, addresses, and telephone numbers of prospects and purchasers. Typically these kiosks are deployed in high-traffic areas within department stores, supermarkets, shopping malls, trade shows, airports, and transportation hubs. Their use is growing rapidly. About 1.5 million installations were reported in 1995.

Unattended merchandising kiosks provide consistent product information, sport attractive displays, and operate twenty-four hours a day without additional cost. They are easily modified to promote and demonstrate new products, engage users in product-related games, dispense coupons, capture names and addresses, accept orders, and process credit purchases.

Because kiosks are exposed to mixed populations and are unattended, certain design characteristics are important:

- Security systems to prevent tampering
- Rugged construction to withstand vandalism
- Ability to handle differing user types
- Ease of operation
- Easily understood messages
- Humor and friendliness of usage
- Rapid information access
- Good touch-screen navigation
- Continuous feedback reassuring the user
- Consistent format of presentations

The average kiosk cost ranges between $10,000 and $15,000, depending on how elaborate the enclosure must be and what special peripherals are included. Project development costs, including acquisition of content materials and authoring, average about $200,000. Transactional kiosks equipped with credit card readers connected to warehousing and dispatching centers require additional software and hardware and are considerably more expensive.

Although all kiosks are stand-alone and unattended, many may be networked with a central control point from which product information is updated. These control points also serve as message receptors, providing current status information for every kiosk on the network. Exhibit 9-6 lists some companies that use kiosks and describes the applications.

Selling-Strategy Advisers

Multimedia-capable notebook computers are a powerful platform for sales automation systems. Traditional applications are territory management, customer database, word processing, forecasting, and communications with corporate data—all text-based applications. More effective selling advisers require multimedia capabilities with images, sound, and videos of product applications and testimonials. Selling advisers to date are simple expert system applications in the product selector category. They match prospect requirements with available products and services but do not provide competitive product analysis.

Selling-strategy advisers are basically interactive multimedia systems designed to dispense instant advice about the optimal selling strategy in a competitive situation. Representatives selling complex products—drugs or sophisticated electronics and industrial equipment, for example—face a monumental task every day of keeping track of the performance and characteristics of each product they sell. The problem is that most people find it impossible to remember comparative data for more than seven factors at a time. Selling advisers handle any number of complex factors for all products involved, with their multimedia output automatically demonstrating the use and features of a product.

Selling strategy advisers can be incorporated into in-house sales training programs as well as deployed on laptop and notebook computers for use in the field. Similar systems can

Exhibit 9-6. Representative merchandising kiosk applications.

Company	Kiosk Application Description
R. Stevens Express	First automated photo machine deployed in drug and grocery stores Films are dropped off and on-screen expert leads the customer through the process of ordering Ælm processing and payment
Chicago White Sox	Developed at Chicago's Comiskey Park Presents trivia games to baseball fans designed to collect demographic information for White Sox marketing department Objective is to develop repeat business by capturing fan names, addresses, and speciÆc interests, with systems disguised as video games
FedEx On-Line	Interactive kiosks for instructing an occasional customer how to send a package through the system Customer can pay with FedEx account number or credit card and receive a receipt as well as routing information through a built-in printer
MUZE/VUZE	A kiosk based on a database of about 100,000 music recordings and 16,000 screen images of album covers deployed in music and record shops Produces a printout with bar codes that identify the music wanted by type, keywords, performers, or albums and facilitate sales by checking availability in stock Some music sampling and video database are being planned for the future.
Emporium Department Stores	Kiosk in store suggests 134 items as Christmas gifts based on inputs from customers about hobbies, interests, and price ranges Includes an expert system coupled with the interactive multimedia application and prints out gift suggestions

be developed for the configuration of complex equipment and comparisons with competitive products on a cost-effective basis.

Selling-Skills Simulators

Selling-skills simulators are complex interactive systems that combine the use of all multimedia elements on a realtime basis and consist of a multimedia platform, as well as a video camera, a microphone, VCR videotapes, and sometimes other videorecording devices, such as rewritable optical disks for storage of videos. These systems present videos of a realistic sales situation and then ask users to defend the product or convince the prospect about the superior qualities for their application. The system records the timed reactions of salespersons, which management then reviews.

> Valuable aspect: The ability to practice until sales personnel reach the best possible response to the most demanding and hostile questions.

Among the regular users are IBM, the CIA, and leading pharmaceutical and financial service organizations.

Portable Multimedia Platforms

Color screen laptops and notebook computers are revolutionizing sales and marketing functions and creating new markets for interactive multimedia applications. These are portable versions of the various sales and marketing concepts already described; because they are portable, they can be left with a client for product or service evaluation. These applications can also replace traditional business presentations consisting of combinations of slides, videotapes, films, and brochures. The interactivity, implied customization, and instant communications capabilities of portable platforms make them clearly superior to traditional marketing devices.

Portable multimedia platforms can take a variety of forms, each with its own capabilities:

- *Portable computer:* Relatively large, integrated unit up to 20 pounds in weight, with a built-in CD-ROM drive, large-capacity hard disk, speakers, microphone, and expansion slots. It provides a large color-active matrix display but is not battery operated and must be plugged in on site.
- *Notebook computer:* Lightweight machines weighing under 10 pounds and battery operated for up to several hours. Multimedia peripherals, such as a CD-ROM drive and speakers, must be attached externally. Some vendors provide docking stations with built-in speakers and CD-ROM drive and additional audio and video boards. Some units include a built-in CD-ROM, but at the expense of other devices.
- *CD-ROM player:* Compact low-cost platform designed as a presentation tool built around a CD-ROM drive and used to display off-the-shelf presentations on relatively small screens. These units are very light, weighing only 2 to 3 pounds, but are much less capable than notebooks and have limited controls or keyboards.
- *CD-I player:* A low-cost device for playing CD-ROM titles used as a peripheral to TV sets and stereo systems. It is primarily designed for interactive video games and music titles but sometimes is used for promotional purposes. These units lack the flexibility of standard PCs and cannot be used to capture market data.
- *Personal digital assistants:* Small, lightweight devices that primarily provide communications functions, including voice, fax, e-mail, paging, touch-screen controls, and wireless connectivity. Currently they do not offer video capabilities, but plans include such features in the future.

Portable multimedia enhances the effectiveness of personal selling with applications on all available products, animated illustrations of how products work, and video testimonials from satisfied customers. On-the-job presentations make sales and service personnel more productive and improve customer satisfaction. They are also used as powerful training platforms for new sales personnel and for introducing new products to existing field forces.

Most often, portable multimedia presentations are based on CD-ROM drives that are attached externally or are built into the portable platform. More effective are corporate networks, local and wide area, that provide immediate access to a multimedia database of information on products, markets, competition, procedures, engineering simulations, or latest prospects and developments. Such multimedia databases can be created on a local server to provide access to many mobile workers in the field through an LAN connection. In the near future, communications networks will handle audio and video traffic, and the servers will be accessed through a built-in modem and portable telephone units. These capabilities will also bring into play integrated conferencing capabilities, which will add to the value of portable multimedia platforms. Exhibit 9-7 illustrates the potential for these concepts.

Notebook computers present the most attractive portable multimedia platform solutions. They are compact, weigh under 10 pounds, and have the power of a desktop with built-in multimedia capabilities. The average 1994 portable had the following characteristics:

- *Central processor:* 486DX4 or Pentium in the range of 75 to over 100 MHz.
- *Memory(RAM):* Minimum 4 MB but 8 MB or more recommended, up to 36 MB.
- *Display:* Active matrix color of 10 inches or larger, with high resolution.
- *Hard disk storage:* Minimum of 250 MB, with up to 680 MB available.
- *CD-ROM drive:* Internal units with double or quadruple speed.
- *Speakers:* Built-in stereo speakers.
- *Audio quality:* Minimum 16-bit sound.
- *Video quality:* Graphics and video accelerators recommended.
- *Weight:* Under 6 pounds.
- *Price:* High-end prices ranging from $5,000 to $8,000.

More than fifty color notebook models on the market are supplied by about two dozen vendors. At least thirty of the

Exhibit 9-7. Potential of portable multimedia platforms.

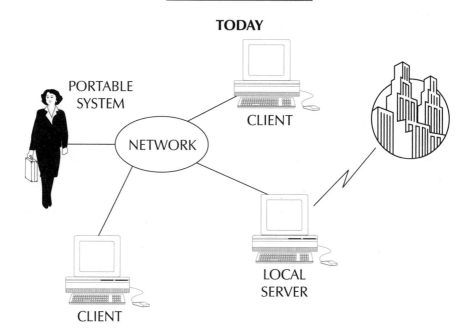

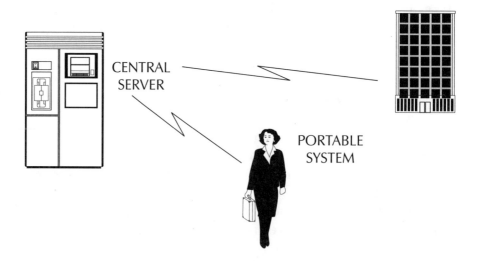

models come with optional docking stations with multimedia peripherals, and sixteen offer CD-ROM drives as options. A few are already integrated with the main unit. Vendors of high-end portable multimedia platforms include Aquiline, Chiplet Systems, Dolch, IBM Personal Computer Co., Panasonic, Texas Instruments, and Toshiba.

Early Adopters

Some of the earliest adopters are industries where customer service is critical both before and after the sale is made. The most successful enterprises in this category are those that give close attention to customer needs and wants. Studies show that customers rate on-time delivery of products and services as more important in making a sale than price. Clearly, service reputation is critical; it is, in fact, second only to product performance.

Before a sale, customer service systems need to identify customer needs and match them with appropriate products. Obviously, the more complex the product is, the more extensive is the service required.

A permanent staff of informed specialists must be on hand to answer customer questions. If they are not available, customers will not wait; they will switch to a supplier with faster response and price quotations.

Interactive multimedia knowledge systems provide information and solutions, handle customers in a consistent manner, and can prequalify prospects for services that require extensive customization, such as insurance policies, financial and investment services, mortgages, and various government services. Their biggest advantage is that they free sales personnel to close sales instead of spending time evaluating and dispensing advice.

Here we look at three adopters of this technology.

Real Estate

Real estate agents know the importance of visual presentations, traditionally accomplished through consuming visits to inspect properties. Some of the earliest attempts at simulated room-by-room property walk-throughs with voice commentary were made in this industry in an effort to reduce the frequency and cost of property inspection and increase salespersons' productivity.

A real estate home shopping network set up by Home View Realty of Needham, Massachusetts, runs a number of search centers in the Boston area. Potential home buyers enter their key criteria—for example, location, price range, architectural style, amenities; nearness to schools, churches, tennis courts, parks, beaches; and others, up to 300 various characteristics—and the system responds with a selection of color images of homes listed by local agents with Home View service. The service, targeted at realty brokers who will list properties at a lower commission rate than usual, intends national expansion.

There are less sophisticated real estate applications as well. One is a touch-screen kiosk in shopping malls that presents images of properties for sale. Electronic Realty Associates of Overland Park, Kansas, is developing a CD-ROM product that allows a user to touch a floor plan of a home and go through a simulated guided tour with voice commentary. Virtual reality technology is also on the minds of real estate promoters and brokers but is still too expensive to produce.

In Denmark, HomeVision, developed by the largest real estate chain in the country, gives buyers the chance to browse through houses for sale and simultaneously collects vital data about family size, location preferences, and financial status.

Real estate property appraisers are using pen-based units or notebook computers to capture data and immediately communicate with central databases for instant updating. The ability to videotape a site and transmit it from the field is of considerable interest but awaits more cost-effective wireless transmission technology.

Insurance Claims

Insurance companies are always seeking new ways to minimize claims processing and judgments that cause unnecessary payments and losses. Interactive multimedia facilitates the investigation and determination of liability in accidents. Such systems depend on simulations in which agents observe accidents and are shown correct liability assessments. Aetna and Allstate are leading developers. Many more insurance companies are also exploring similar approaches.

Financial Services

Because of the immense value of information in the financial services industry, it is among early technology adopters.

Financial services include two basic categories: the trading floor, functioning in near realtime, and analytical and corporate clients, who can research markets, ventures, and companies. All services are based on providing information whose content comes from the same sources and is limited in amount at any given time. Products are differentiated through analysis, presentation, speed of delivery, and quality of service. Creative use of interactive technology facilitates communication of ideas and comprehension of financial situations.

Video broadcasts from Financial News Network (FNN), Cable News Network (CNN), Knight-Ridder, and other sources are delivered directly to broker or trader workstations. Among the leading financial service providers are Bloomberg Financial, Dow Jones, and Reuters Holdings. Bloomberg Financial provides access to audio and images on proprietary terminals and is developing interactive video for 36,000 business subscribers worldwide.

The Dow Jones Investor Network, launched in 1993, provides video news, interviews, and live press conferences directly to PCs equipped with PS/2 TV devices. Video distribution uses coaxial cable routed through a TokenRing local area network. Dow Jones also is developing an interactive multimedia version with NYNEX, and its Telerate supplies video for trading floor customers.

Reuters Holdings launched a video service to PCs targeted at foreign exchange traders. And Reuters New Media, formed in January 1994, looks for opportunities in nontraditional markets, such as interactive cable TV, health care, and education.

The use of a voice-controlled trading workstation to enhance trader productivity is jointly sponsored by Citibank, First

Boston, Goldman Sachs, Morgan Stanley, Salomon Brothers, and Shearson. Additionally, attempts have been made to introduce virtual reality—which simulates relationships between various variables in a graphic manner—to presentations of complex financial relationships that change on a realtime basis.

Financial institutions serving consumer markets—banks and investment, mortgage, and insurance firms—are exploring interactive multimedia solutions as ways to reduce waiting lines, provide more competitive services, and train employees efficiently. Some banks are considering expansion of automatic teller machines to include insurance, investments, mutual funds, and travel services.

Travel Industry

SABREvision, developed by American Airlines and deployed by more than a thousand travel agencies, is one of the best examples in the industry. The system provides maps of destinations, images of hotel lobbies and rooms, and other local details. National Car Rental Systems and Budget Rent-a-Car use interactive multimedia booths to handle car rentals without the intervention of counter personnel. And the moving industry uses Ryder Touch-TV, an interactive merchandising system, to provide information about new locations, comparative living costs, and packing lists.

Spotlight on the Future

Rapid price reduction and simultaneous enhancement of portable color screen notebooks as interactive multimedia platforms are resulting in increased sales forces automation. Powerful low-cost portable videoconferencing workstations are technically possible today; their commercialization awaits the availability of high-bandwidth digital-switched network services.

In consumer markets, interactive TV is a major user and promoter of multimedia, including interactive advertising, but it is not expected to grow as fast or become as large as predicted. It remains uncertain as to whether consumers will want to select and buy goods remotely from virtual shopping centers rather shop at the actual locations. Pilot tests are continuing to provide information. There is considerable use of online services and the Internet World Wide Web to present small graphic and video advertisements but their success depends on availability of good lines to Web sources.

10

Making Better Business Presentations

Multimedia comes into its own with professional business presentations. Companies that use multimedia for these presentations will garner more attention and be perceived as more professional than their competitors stuck with the traditional presentation tools. As global competition intensifies, speed and accuracy assume enormous importance. Multimedia provides the fastest, cheapest, and easiest way to reach clients, customers, and partners. Businesses that do not adopt interactive multimedia communications may perish.

The highest-quality presentations must be developed, because each will be competing in the open market with many other presentations.

A Business Research Group study shows that 85 percent of business presentations already use multimedia technology. In 1994, a Dataquest survey found that business presentations accounted for at least 40 percent of all multimedia applications and represented the largest single multimedia market segment. Analysts believe business presentations will remain the mainstay of multimedia industry for many years to come.

There are a number of reasons for the position of business presentations in multimedia use:

- growth in number and quality of cost-effective platforms
- explosion of mobile multimedia computing
- increasing interest in desktop videoconferencing
- a competitive environment of interactive multimedia de-

velopers equipped with cost-effective multimedia authoring and development tools

Dynamics of Human Communications

An effective business presentation begins by capturing the attention of the user or target audience. Multimedia presentations do this best because they engage all of the senses.

Recall the statistics already presented on communications: that spoken words alone account for only 7 percent of the total impact of face-to-face encounters. More significant are voice tone and inflection, accounting for 38 percent of the total impact in an encounter. More important still are the visual aspects of body language—including gestures and facial expressions—which provide 55 percent of the total communications impact (Exhibit 10-1).

Exhibit 10-1. Interactive communications dynamics.

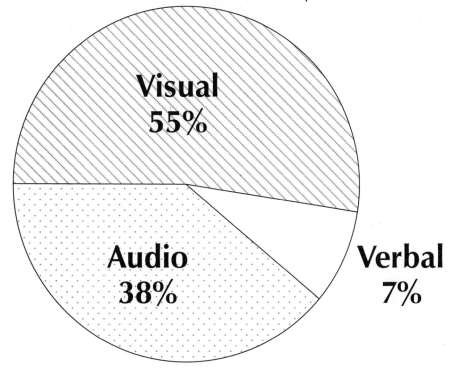

Benefits of Multimedia Presentations

Multimedia business presentations are faster, cheaper, easier, and better than conventional alternatives. Moreover, they combine motion and sound and engage the human senses on several levels—verbal, voice, and visual—simultaneously. The user feels closer to the information being communicated and experiences a multisensory process similar to actual life.

Digital systems and content materials eliminate costs involved in alternative presentations such as 35-mm cameras, film, slide preparation, videotapes, and additional analog materials. Once a business presentation is digitally encoded and stored, duplicating costs are minimal. Direct delivery of the business presentation in digital form is easier to deliver and eliminates the need to manipulate other media and equipment—particularly costly, time-consuming, and error prone when dealing with printed and published media. It is also easy to update, expand, and distribute. The upshot is that better business presentation solutions are being developed faster in response to, and in anticipation of, competitive action. The results are clear:

- *Faster development.* Multimedia technologies permit faster development of business presentations with dynamic sound and video components.
- *Cheaper production.* Digital systems and content eliminate costs associated with 35-mm film, slides, videotape, and other analog materials providing direct output from a computer. Cost of duplication of presentations electronically is minimal.
- *Easier delivery.* Direct delivery of business presentations from a computer eliminates the need to manipulate other media and equipment. Once set up, it is easy to update and expand.
- *Better solutions.* Multimedia presentations can result in higher sales, more new business, improved corporate image, enhanced credibility, better order response, and improved customer service and relations.

MIS managers who are aware of sources of information on business presentations in general, and multimedia specifically, will ᴛ e prepared to meet existing and forthcoming challenges.

Business Presentation Categories

Although business presentations styles and techniques vary, all have the same objective: to persuade one or more individuals to take an action. Multimedia components can strengthen any conventional presentation and introduce added persuasiveness through interactivity and customization.

The following major business presentations can benefit from multimedia applications:

- *Annual meetings.* Large public audiences require special screens and projection equipment. Heavy video, graphics, and animation use contribute to the presentation.
- *Boardroom presentations.* Small, high-level audiences require heavy use of graphics and animation to illustrate corporate performance.
- *Dealer and sales meetings.* Large audiences require special screens and projectors, although the presentation may be implemented on PC desktops and portable platforms equipped with multimedia capabilities. Product demonstration and user testimonial videos can be important.
- *Press conferences.* These generally small presentations combine videos of executive spokespersons and corporate performance data. They can draw on materials developed for other corporate presentations.
- *Conventions.* Special booth or seminar presentations introduce new products or technologies and present corporate policy to prospects, clients, and investors.
- *Trade exhibits.* Specialized product and technology demonstrations during exhibitions can be attended or unattended kiosks.
- *Merchandising kiosks.* Information on transactional touchscreen kiosks can be deployed in high-traffic public areas or corporate campuses.
- *World Wide Web.* Mostly promotional home pages pro-

vide corporate and product information with interconnectivity to related products and services.

- *Training.* Although a category in itself, many training sessions are in support of product and service sales and use materials from all other corporate presentations.

An added benefit is that digital elements created for one presentation are useful in many other events. Thanks to digital storage and transmission, such activity can significantly accelerate production and reduce the cost of other business presentations. Multimedia business presentations are easier to perform in several ways. The visuals are computer screens stored inside the memory or a CD-ROM disk and do not require recording on another medium. Once a system is tested and running, it is easy to control.

Comforting reward: There is no need to set up, synchronize, and operate several separate analog playback devices.

Above all, multimedia makes it easier to communicate ideas and messages to audiences. Often a 30-second video clip with audio commentary can replace minutes of lengthy descriptive text and diagrams. It is easy to add to or modify an existing electronic presentation. In the long run, multimedia presentations are faster, cheaper, and easier to implement than conventional presentations.

The World Wide Web provides a means to promote products and services to millions. Businesses find it attractive because the cost of sale on the Internet is about two cents compared to about five dollars through conventional mail order. Moreover, the number of users is skyrocketing from 3 million in 1995 to an anticipated 10 million by 1997 and 22 million by the year 2000.

Internet and Web users are not specifically tied to any particular subject or service, and they are free to surf cyberspace in search of the most intriguing and compelling presentations. Clearly, presentation distinction is important. This activity will intensify through the use of specialized intelligent search agents.

For those seeking effective business presentation ideas, the Web is an excellent research and evaluation resource. New ventures and services offering periodic lists and addresses are the Web sites visited the most. Trade periodicals conduct contests for the best Web home pages and provide excellent sources of information for the creation of successful business presentations.

Planning a Business Presentation

Those new to multimedia development often mistakenly rush to the first available authoring system when the first step is outlining a plan. The plan should take into account multimedia content, development tools, design options, and interactivity and impact choices.

> Most important: The plan starts with a needs analysis and audience assessment.

The development process presents a tremendous freedom of choice but, paradoxically, requires strict planning for the best results. Veteran multimedia developers suggest that half of the designing and business presentation efforts be completed *before* using authoring software.

Four phases are basic to the planning process:

1. *Analyze target audiences.* This is the most critical aspect of a business presentation needs analysis because it provides detailed demographics about the end users.
2. *Determine presentation objectives.* Is the presentation to inform, promote, sell, train, educate, or entertain? These objectives will influence the choice of content, media, and delivery and define the budget.
3. *Assess available resources.* This step encompasses assessing the existing and readily available hardware, software, programming, and creative skills and determining overall budgets and delivery deadlines.
4. *Develop the plan of action for production.* Use an overall decision tree of the presentation and all its branches,

with specific text, graphics, audio, and video segments assigned to specific task groups or outside specialists.

Traditional journalism questions should precede the design:

- *Who.* Who is the targeted audience? What are its demographics and their attitudes?
- *What.* What is the specific content that is being conveyed to the audience, and in what context is it being presented?
- *When.* At what time of the working day will the presentation be delivered?
- *Where.* What type of venue is being contemplated for delivery of the presentation? Venue may vary from a large auditorium to conference rooms and individual PCs, both private and public in nature.
- *Why.* What are the goals and objectives of this presentation?
- *How.* What resources are available to undertake the project in terms of budget and deadlines (time and money)?

Top-notch business presentations will result only with the skillful use of technology by professional multimedia applications developers. Corporate managers are often put in a situation where they must make decisions dealing with unfamiliar subjects, topics, and skills. In this area, a common mistake is the outright purchase of an authoring system and assigning it to a programmer for development. But remember that multimedia presentations are a special form. Their quality depends on a skillful combination of voice, video, images, animation, and text—by an expert. Either the information technology staff must be specially trained, or a creative person with an aptitude for using computers and authoring tools is hired. Both courses of action are being pursued by a growing number of companies and training and educational institutions.

The Needs Analysis

The needs analysis should be undertaken before any funding or delivery commitments are made. It should:

1. Define the objectives.
2. Appraise the targeted audiences to determine their characteristics.
3. Assess the delivery environment because it determines the operational parameters within which the multimedia application must function. Particularly critical, if networked transactions are being planned, is ensuring sufficient bandwidth to handle traffic without degradation of networking operations. Nothing is worse than business presentations transmitted out of sync or with video images that are too small, jittery, and annoying to watch.
4. Formalize the conceptual design in the form of a storyboard outlining. This is comparable to a proposal for an interactive movie or TV commercial and is one of the best ways to convey the overall project and its logical information flow to all concerned.

Time and Cost Estimates

Digital presentations provide output directly from a computer, so savings multiply when presentations are duplicated. In the case of multimedia presentations, it boils down to a diskette or a CD-ROM whose reproduction costs are nominal. In the future, the only cost may be that of transmission from a server to a portable presentation or videoconferencing terminal.

An interactive multimedia presentation that runs for an hour usually contains about 100 to 120 individual screens. However, screens vary in complexity, and construction may take anywhere from 15 minutes to several hours. It all depends on how many different text, graphics, animation, audio, video, and navigational control objects are involved. Each screen should be documented with its own design to keep track of its development and any subsequent changes and design responsibilities throughout the project life cycle.

The overall presentation is best completed and documented with a decision-tree flowchart relating individual screens to each other and identifying all interactivity. The decision tree is like a map that all members of the design team can use to understand their specific roles and to measure progress.

It is comparable to flow charts in conventional systems analysis, except that it includes elements of text, graphics, audio, video, and animation as part of the process.

Once planning activities are complete, it is possible to determine the most useful authoring systems and software needed to build and test the system. By now, delivery facilities influencing types of software are known. It is a mistake to acquire tools before all the parameters are defined and the needs analysis completed. The rest is a trade-off between quality of output and available resources.

Delivery Modes

The proper delivery environment makes or breaks even the best presentation. A variety of delivery modes exists, with new ones being introduced regularly. For example, notebook computers with detachable transparent screens can be projected onto a large screen using overhead projectors. With a larger audience, the screen design must be appropriate to make sure text and images are large enough to be clear to people sitting in the back row.

Each monitor and projector has advantages and limitations. All aspects must be considered before a final choice is made.

Pure multimedia, interactive CD-ROM-based business presentations represent a relatively small segment of the business presentation market, which is currently dominated by videotapes, overheads, and slides. Traditional methods account for about 75 percent of the market. Slides are the largest single segment and experiencing growth with the new software for production. Nevertheless, this market is estimated at over $23 billion—a huge potential for multimedia technology incorporation.

Development Tools

It takes as long to create a multimedia presentation with current authoring tools as it does a black-and-white overhead transparency presentation.

Bottom-line reward: The required time, price of authoring tools, and learning time invested pay off with a fast
return on investment, making the effort worthwhile.

Software presentation tools come in three categories: (1)
traditional charting and outlining programs used to create slide
shows, (2) advanced packages designed to integrate multimedia elements into presentations, and (3) time-line-based software for sequencing audio and video content. A single tool that
provides powerful multimedia synchronization features for all
types of content does not exist yet.

When you evaluate tools, these are the most important features:

- usability
- graphics capability
- outlining and charting features
- media integration and editing
- synchronization capabilities
- inclusion of transition effects
- animation
- interactivity
- run-time fees
- cross-platform portability

The presentation market holds a huge potential for vendors of easy-to-use tools. If authoring can be made as simple as
word processing, all computer users would use such products.
Vendors of presentation authoring tools fall into three groups,
catering to specific end users:

1. *Traditional presentation products* focus on charting—an
   important function in all business presentations. Vendors include Lotus Development with Freelance Graphics, Software Publishing with Harvard Graphics, and
   Microsoft with PowerPoint. These products command
   large market shares, and their standards are being followed by other vendors, which are providing specific
   features not initially available within the traditional
   products.

2. *Animation tools* appeal more to artistic and creative developers, but they are not the easiest to use and may not offer other functions important to presentation development. Vendors include Autodesk, Gold Disk, and Vividus.

3. *Media integration products* represent the fastest-growing segment, with programs that maximize flexibility of importing and combining different media formats into a smooth-running presentation. The leading vendors are Asymetrix, IBM, and Macromedia. Small ventures are entering the market with competing products, and the field is getting crowded.

Exhibit 10-2 lists the more popular multimedia business presentation tools.

Presentation authoring tools have evolved from simple chart-creating programs to more comprehensive systems with integration capabilities. The most significant trend is object oriented, with every presentation element treated as an object with specific test, audio, and animation properties. The purpose is to make these tools so easy to use that users can concentrate entirely on content creation.

Exhibit 10-2. Major multimedia presentation tools.

Tool Vendor	Presentation Software	Telephone
Adobe Systems	Aldus Persuasion 3.0	(800) 628-2320
Alpha	Bravo 2.0	(800) 451-1018
Ask Me Multimedia	Super Show & Tell 2.0	(800) 275-6311
Asymetrix	Compel 2.0	(800) 448-6543
Gold Disk	Astound 1.01 (Mac)	(800) 982-9888
	Astound 2.0 (Win)	
Lotus Development	Freelance Graphics 2.1	(800) 343-5414
Macromedia Design	Action 1.0.4 (Mac)	(800) 288-4797
	Action 3.0 (Win)	
Micrografx	Charisma 4.0	(800) 758-1985
Microsoft	PowerPoint 4.0	(800) 426-9400
Multimedia Design	mPower 2.0	(704) 523-9493
Q/Media	Q/Media 2.0	(800) 444-9356
Software Publishing	Harvard Graphics 3.0	(800) 234-2500
Wordperfect (Novell)	WP Presentation 3.0	(800) 451-5151

Spotlight on the Future

The need to support cross-platform solutions will grow as multimedia presentations increase. Presentations will be run on a variety of platforms without additional reprogramming. Sophisticated scripting languages and visual metaphors that can be used by anyone are currently under development. Increasing support is also being given to multimedia data types in various hardware and software environments. Client-server and networking environments also require the development of presentation authoring tools to allow collaborative group authoring. We need better functions within the tools to facilitate updating. To make complex tools easier to use, inclusion of intelligent agents based on artificial intelligence techniques is in the research and development pipeline. Voice recognition technology is expected to improve end-user interface.

11

Collaborative Work Group Computing: Getting Everybody Into the Act

Work group computing, the basis of collaborative interactive multimedia communications, occurs when several workers transmit information to each other simultaneously, comment on it, and manipulate the data or images.

Work group computing can take place with or without video. If transmission of working information is the main objective, video images of participants add little to the process. If the collaboration involves explanations of, say, product designs, mechanisms, or chemical structures, then video is valuable.

Collaborative Computing: What It's All About

Collaborative work with cross-functional development teams is an effective way to shorten product development cycles. A McKinsey study reveals that companies lose 33 percent of their after-tax profits when they ship products six months late. On the other hand, if they overspend, by even as much as 50 percent, on product development, the losses come to 3.5 percent—almost ten times less. As a result, companies are looking to work group and collaborative computing to reduce product development cycles and contribute to competitiveness in global markets.

There are five major functions of collaborative computing:

1. *E-mail*—the most popular and powerful mechanism for communication of information among end users. It has potential for audio and video annotation.
2. *Work group management*—for creating group schedules, assigning group deadlines, evaluating performance, and scheduling meetings, projects, tasks, and work flow deadlines, as well as of staff, resources, and equipment.
3. *Shared documents*—for providing concurrent access to stored documents and images. Document manipulation tools are used for the creation, editing, reviewing, publishing, storing, and deleting of multimedia objects.
4. *Work flow automation*—for facilitating route information among workers according to special business rules.
5. *Conferencing*—for videoconferencing facilities, computerized whiteboards, and individual workstations; electronic voting, brainstorming, and recording in face-to-face or remote meetings; and desktop conferencing, shared electronic whiteboards, and shared computer applications.

The most popular of these activities is e-mail, which in many instances possesses audio and video annotation capabilities. E-mail is a powerful mechanism for information communications throughout a collaborating group and does not require the simultaneous presence of all the members. On the other hand, e-mail and work flow tools tend to create "cyberglut" because it is so easy to broadcast information to many users, whether it is wanted, useful, and relevant or not. More interactive group activities, like realtime telephones and videoconferencing, produce immediate feedback, which has the effect of filtering our irrelevant or unwanted information.

Caution: When overwhelming amounts of irrelevant e-mail arrive and go unread, it loses its advantage as a work group tool. Agent technology is being developed to discard unwanted messages into an automatic electronic wastebasket.

E-mail's future lies in the integration of existing systems with voice and video annotation and fax services; all use telephone networks for connectivity. Interactive videomail eventually will replace such individual services by a single-server system that can handle all functions. When this happens, users can receive messages in whatever form they arrive or choose a format regardless of the original input. Interoperable documents can then be sent out in one form and received in another (see Exhibit 11-1). Some products are now on the market, and more will appear as the information superhighway expands.

Facilitating Work Group Computing

Work group computing uses hardware and software products that enable extensive networking. It also employs object technologies, client-servers, multimedia databases, and associated peripherals that facilitate the implementation of collaborative computing at group, department, and enterprise levels.

Object-oriented Technologies

Object-oriented technology is based on the concept that the world consists of objects with defined and distinct characteristics and behaviors. Object-oriented software products provide the tools to accumulate, manipulate, and distribute objects and are suitable for collaborative multimedia computing. They allow easy development and modification of systems that depend on a variety of changing sources of data, images, and sounds rather than structured numerical and textual data. Multimedia content elements used to assemble multimedia applications are, in fact, digital objects of various sizes that are integrated together in various ways. Multimedia authoring systems are excellent examples of object-oriented technology in use. Exhibit 11-2 displays these objects.

Object software products enable workers who are using a variety of computer platforms in different locations to work col-

Exhibit 11-1. Interoperable videomail concept.

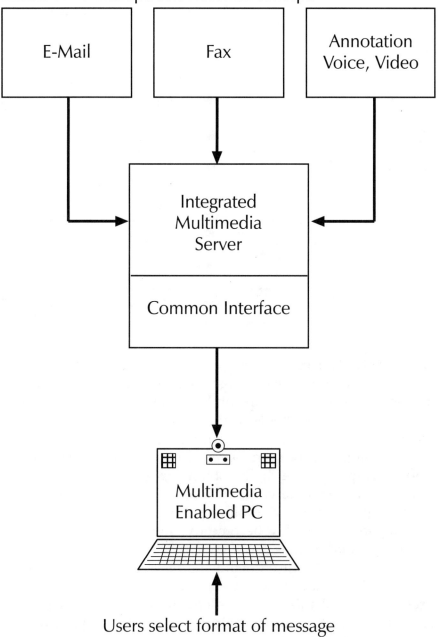

Exhibit 11-2. Multimedia objects.

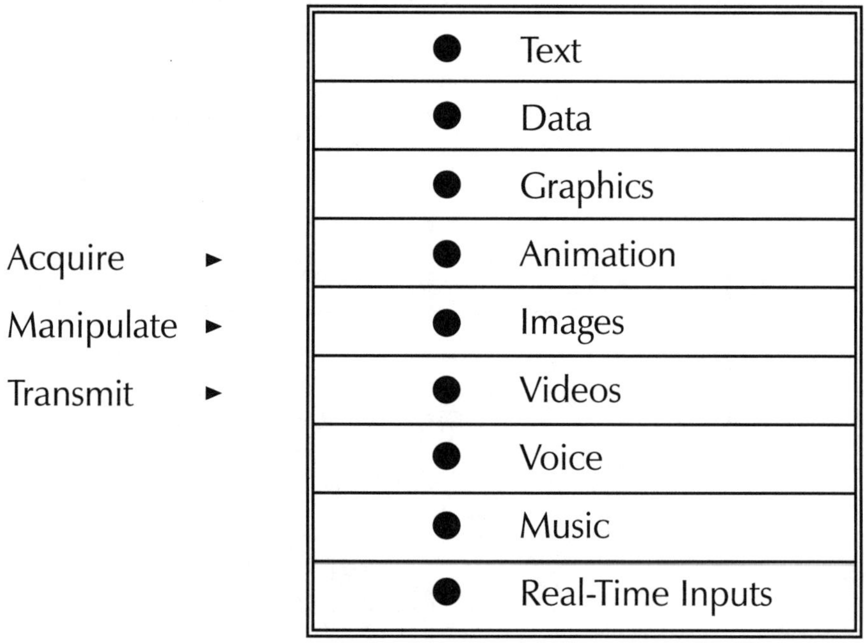

●	Text
●	Data
●	Graphics
●	Animation
●	Images
●	Videos
●	Voice
●	Music
●	Real-Time Inputs

Acquire ▶

Manipulate ▶

Transmit ▶

laboratively. Object technology assists teamwork and allows geographically dispersed designers, manufacturing executives, and accountants to develop and bring new products to market.

Object-oriented tools include programming languages, databases, data managers, authoring systems, and some artificial intelligence and expert systems. These tools are used to develop and manipulate digital objects, which can take the form of content elements or combinations of basic objects into complete screens and programming routines.

Documents quickly become dynamic, modular, multimedia objects, and as files proliferate, they become containers for the documents. Because documents represent 80 percent of all corporate information, document management is important for keeping track of intellectual assets. Electronic documents can contain information about their origin and identity, as well as execute codes that manipulate and render them.

Eventually future operating systems will offer universal object storage capabilities to handle documents, messages, data records, and program modules. Document management systems are more dynamic than document imaging products. Document imaging systems move and handle fixed files. Management systems know an original document, who looks at it, and when; they allow editing and rendering, which may change the document's appearance depending on how it was accessed. Object-oriented tools and products are summarized in Exhibit 11-3.

Desktop Systems

Many stand-alone and portable PCs are equipped with basic features for multimedia delivery based on CD-ROM technologies: audio and video boards, CD-ROM drives, and speakers. For work group computing, desktops must be networked in LAN environments, many without enough bandwidth for effective transmission.

Desktop multimedia systems are designed for stand-alone

Exhibit 11-3. Object-oriented technologies.

Object Products	Description of Functions
Languages and tools	Programming languages such as C++ and Small Talk and associated utilities that allow development of reusable software code modeling real-world objects and processes
	Operating systems designed for handling objects
Developer's tools	Object class libraries
	Graphical user interfaces (GUIs)
	Authoring systems
	Expert systems
	Multimedia data managers
	Application frameworks
Object databases	Store and manipulate abstract data types, such as voice, video, animation, graphics, and large multimedia Æles
	Handle complex objects for modeling and simulation applications
CASE products	A special class of object tools for developing complex applications in large software systems

individual delivery of interactive multimedia training programs for business presentations. Multimedia applications are delivered by physical distribution of CD-ROM disks with specific programs. Theoretically, any PC platform can be upgraded to handle multimedia applications by adding hardware peripherals and operating software. In fact, there is significant potential for incompatibility. This issue can be minimized if the PCs used by work groups have identical platforms, but this is seldom the case.

The existence of multimedia-capable desktops within a group does not automatically mean that work group computing can take place. You must analyze the platforms with regard to their capabilities and upgrade them to a minimum standard sufficient to support the multimedia collaborative system.

Group-Level Networks

Interaction is the key to work group computing. It exists in many forms at various levels within a corporation. Normally there is a gradual progression from relatively simple user access to electronic documents, through user creation and manipulation of electronic files, to user-to-user collaboration through videoconferencing and other groupware systems.

Phasing in Networks

When individual platforms are upgraded to handle multimedia applications, group multimedia networking develops in stages:

1. The first phase provides individual users with access to multimedia files resident in databases, client-servers, or specialized video servers. Multimedia collaboration is not yet feasible, but some of the LAN segments can be upgraded to carry multimedia traffic. The initial users are usually in-house multimedia developers who are building corporate multimedia applications for distribution through CD-ROM or magnetic disk media and require access to permanent multimedia and document imaging repositories. This is the time to assess the needs of other users and determine network architectures and bandwidth ca-

pacities required to implement group networking within the enterprise.

2. In phase 2, LANs are used to distribute multimedia applications or video presentations to enabled desktops in the company. This is a one-to-many broadcasting mode that may use existing LANs and cable networks and does not require two-way realtime interactivity. Time-sensitive video components are downloaded to local client-servers, video servers, or even suitably equipped individual PCs for retrieval and use at a time convenient to each end user. At this stage, many desktops on the LAN may not have network links with sufficient bandwidth capacity to support conferencing.

3. In the third phase, realtime work group computing develops on corporate LANs in the form of local groupware applications that initially handled only text and data. These include e-mail, work group management, sharing of documents, work flow automation, and some forms of teleconferencing. At this stage, work group computing may be implemented using alternative architectures such as file sharing, databases, or message routing.

In file sharing, the shared information is stored on LAN servers in one or more files. Files are locked when a user adds or modifies its content. This simplest solution exploits network operating system administrative and security features. The users must be directly connected to the LAN, so this architecture is not suitable for handling remote users.

In databases, the shared information is stored in RDBMS or other databases, and there is concurrent and version management of shared documents. This system tracks users of shared documents and locks at the document level. Database connectivity is required except when replication support is available.

Message routing is an e-mail system that delivers shared information to users across the LAN. This activity can be combined with file sharing or database architectures. Message routing supports remote users, multiple network operating systems, and user platforms. But it is complex in administration and hard to determine the currency of specific information, there are message delivery delays across WANs, and routed documents are not available to other users.

The most sophisticated work group computing networks may combine elements of all the possible architectures. Whatever the approach, upgrading such groupware systems to multimedia conferencing requires enabling the LANs to handle realtime video transmissions.

Scheduling

Collaborative applications such as multiuser videoconferencing are subject to two limitations: the difficulty of scheduling more than a few users at the same time and differences in time zones, countries, or continents. The success of collaborative group conferencing depends on efficient work group scheduling using e-mail and work group management functions well in advance.

Typically not all required participants will take part in the scheduled conference. Surveys suggest that the probability of a person's participating during the next seven days is 80 percent. This means that if more than eight participants are scheduled, the chances of a successful collaborative session are relatively low. When ten workers are involved, the probability drops to 11 percent, and with twenty-five people it is under 0.5 percent.

Time zone differences create scheduling problems, particularly when a conference takes place among participants in Australia, Europe, and North America. A possible solution is to provide massive store-and-forward systems so other participants can review recorded conferencing sessions after the sessions are over. This requires security measures governing access to storage, limiting how long sessions should be stored, and a means for purging the information.

LANs, WANs, and Other Options

The crucial aspects of enterprise-wide multimedia systems are the bandwidth and throughput capabilities of LANs and WANs. Alternative solutions have emerged in corporate environments that require restructuring existing LAN architectures. Network managers face an increasing number of high-speed alternatives depending on existing LAN facilities, cabling, and distances between group participants. (Exhibit 11-4 lists the options.)

Not all of the alternatives support realtime interactive video because the primary objective of high-speed LANs is to relieve text and data traffic congestion on existing networks. Network managers wanting to protect investments in Ethernet LANs expand bandwidth capacity by selecting Ethernet-related solutions. However, FDDI is probably the most effective interim solution and ATM the ultimate multimedia traffic solution.

Exhibit 11-4. Multimedia networking options.

Option	Bandwidth	Characteristics and Comments
LAN Segments	10 Mbps	Uses star topology to turn each user into a LAN segment. Not suitable for realtime video
isoENET	10 Mbps data 6Mbps video	Uses standard Ethernet LAN with additional video channel and ISDN links. Supports realtime video to the desktop
Fast Ethernet 100VG-AnyLAN	100 Mbps	Uses demand priority for handling multimedia trafÆc. Not suitable for realtime interactive video transmission
FDDI	100 Mbps	Based on Æber-optic token ring architecture. Not suitable for realtime interactive video transmissions
ATM	25-51 Mbps	Uses Æxed cell-based switching. Ideal for realtime interactive video and any other data transmissions.
ATM	155 Mbps and over	Ideal for backbone and WAN networks. Supports realtime interactive video and any other data on an internetwork basis

A recent CIMI study determined that the maximum throughput for corporate networking during the rest of the 1990s is about 27 Mbps. This is based on the assumption that the network will carry eight simultaneous video sessions requiring 1.5 Mbps each and other data traffic, for which 15 Mbps should suffice. The video transmissions will require 1.5 Mbps on the assumption that MPEG-2 compression standards will be in use, allowing for full-screen video display. Considering that it is very hard to schedule more than eight participants to a conference of any kind at the same time, this assumption appears to be a realistic estimate. How soon communicating multimedia platforms will all support MPEG-2 compression is another matter.

Concurrent Engineering

Concurrent or simultaneous engineering is a special form of group activity dealing with specific project or product development. It combines desktop conferencing, multimedia file sharing, and multimedia databases. Traditionally, various stages of a design and manufacturing process are performed by different groups. Massive volumes of data are generated, and they must be transmitted from work group to work group. The potential for error is significant.

As more complex CAD/CAM systems, 3-D modelers, and rendering systems appeared, integration of these files into a common database became imperative. Simultaneously, the need to handle binary large objects, images, and files led to the development of object databases. Powerful UNIX workstation LANs were used to coordinate the product design process between all work groups: clients, marketing, financing, design engineers, manufacturing, customer service, and maintenance. As a result, this collaborative concept developed into concurrent engineering, which is considered one of the most promising applications of multiuser multimedia technology.

Concurrent engineering requires significant changes in corporate cultures, but the benefits make it mandatory. Exhibit 11-5 illustrates the time and cost savings from using concurrent engineering. Interactive multimedia networking is the facilitat-

Exhibit 11-5. Concurrent engineering concept.

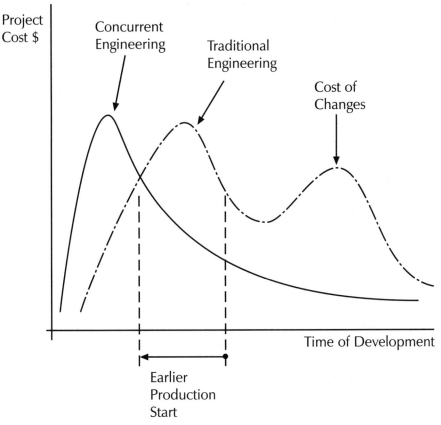

ing technology that accelerates the introduction of concurrent engineering.

Multimedia Databases

Multimedia networking imposes special demands on database management systems. Digitized content such as videos, images, animation, and sounds require massive amounts of storage space. It is also time-consuming to analyze and select materials when looking for content to fit an application. A multimedia database is the logical solution. But although many conventional databases can handle multimedia data types, they are not easy to use and require extensive investment in programming.

Multimedia databases are software systems that store data

types such as text, images, audio, and video. These files can be manipulated and changed by the end user through a workstation or a PC. Databases are designed using RDBMSs that handle multimedia data types; object databases, suited for complex object manipulation, including all multimedia data types; or hybrid database systems that combine RDBMS and object databases. All RDBMS vendors include multimedia capabilities in their products. Eventually most RDBMS products will include storage and client-server development capacilities or options.

Object databases are suited to multimedia applications development because they handle complex data types, such as video images, audio, and graphics—tasks that traditional RDBMS cannot as yet always accomplish. In an object database, the user can store and retrieve data such as video clips and can structure and manipulate contents.

During the application development process, a need exists to identify, inspect, and select large quantities of multimedia content materials. These materials may also exist on CD-ROMs, video and tape cassettes, slides, books, and publications. This work is most often performed by art directors and designers, who are not programmers and often are not able to use complex multimedia databases. As a result, special products known as **multimedia data managers** (sometimes incorrectly labeled as multimedia databases) accomplish these tasks.

Data manager applications are basically cataloging systems designed to facilitate searching and sorting of multimedia materials. Most provide facilities to inspect audio, video, and image files in several ways, such as viewing of thumbnail images, individual previews, and descriptions of the actual multimedia files, their characteristics and locations.

Client-Servers

Client-server technology provides the basic infrastructure that makes interactive multimedia networking and communications possible. Client-server infrastructures are critical to networking applications and more important than other related technologies. Networked applications are hard to justify without appropriate client-server architecture in place. Client-server computing provides a number of benefits facilitating networked multimedia, including realtime collaborative multimedia conferencing. Client-server environments also provide access to databases and multimedia resources, relieving the end user from the need to match his or her individual platform capabilities with traffic requirements. An important client-server feature is scalability. Additional client-servers can be brought online as work group computing expands. They also provide complete platform independence and a means of rapid response to changing market and business conditions. Client-server architectures enabling realtime interactive capabilities are necessary environments for the development of the virtual corporation, seen as tomorrow's most strategic competitive weapon. Traffic solutions involve special video servers, distinct from database servers and file servers, linked by a backbone LAN system.

Client-server technology is not cheap and is not implemented as a cost-cutting measure. Besides client-server hardware and software, additional costs are new applications, end-user training and support, wiring, and communications. As a result over 70 percent of client-server investment represents labor and consulting assistance. Savings can be achieved by limiting client-server technology investments to a few standardized systems and devices with known interoperability. Another area of savings is to automate labor-intensive tasks like software distribution and backup systems.

Client-server technology, a rapid increase in LAN traffic, and the introduction of multimedia applications are the three factors driving the need for high-speed networks. Document imaging and growth in LAN networking or WANs are also significant contributing factors. The initial cost of new networking technologies, the need to rewire networking infrastructures, the complexity of integration with existing LANs, inadequate network management systems, and the resulting risk of downtime in strategic applications are major barriers. A client-server multimedia solution for a LAN with an FDDI backbone ring is illustrated in Exhibit 11-6.

Early Adopters

For almost a decade groupware applications have been synonymous with Lotus Notes, installed in about 5 million applica-

Exhibit 11-6. Multimedia client-server architecture.

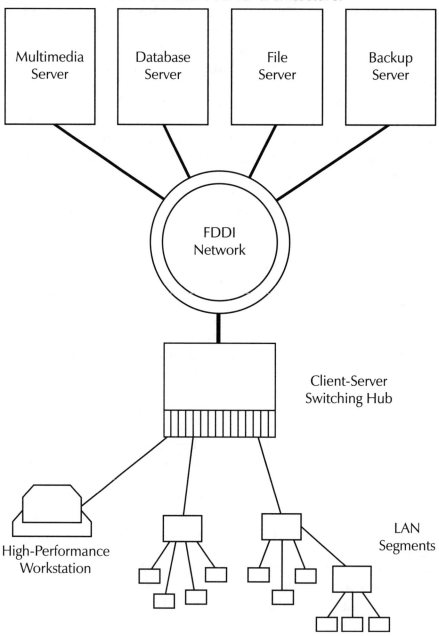

tions. Since then, new vendors have offered products that provide different levels of work group functions, including multimedia data manipulation and transmission. Exhibit 11-7 summarizes a few cases of groupware applications that use multimedia data transmissions and storage.

Exhibit 11-7. Typical work group applications with multimedia.

End User	Groupware Application
Warner Brothers Imaging Technology	Creation, development, and production of digitized cartoons. Very high-quality video requires high-speed LAN/WAN links with a minimum 622 Mbps bandwidth to support transmissions of 24-bit color images and video comparable to movie-theater quality with 50-foot screens. System uses ATM switches from Fore Systems.
Virginia Neurological Institute	Videoconferencing already allows physicians to share X-ray and medical images. A Æber-optic link is used to connect with outside hospitals. VNI is establishing a Neurological Visualization Laboratory in which doctors can examine 3-D images from all over the country. Use of ATM LAN based on Newbridge Networks switches.
BDM International	Conducts teleconferences three times a week among engineers from a dozen-member defense contractor consortium. A central meeting agenda is posted, and document objects can be linked to it and shared during a meeting. Uses Virtual Notebook System and MCI Communications teleconferencing linking PCs, Macs, and UNIX platforms.
General Services Administration	Glenn Asset Management Information System (GAMIS) manages 16,000 government properties in thirteen databases and includes photographs of buildings and details about occupying agencies. Based on Lotus Notes connected to a geographic information system and an expert system running under OS/2 and Compaq servers in Washington, D.C., and ten regional centers.

Specialized Vendors

There are at least three dozen vendors with over sixty groupware–work flow products on the market. Of those, over twenty
products include document and image management features
that support multimedia data structures. Only a few support
audio and videoconferencing features and shared screens.
Leading groupware software vendors are Lotus Development,
Digital Equipment, Oracle, and Teamware Division of ICL. Of
those, DEC's LinkWorks, Lotus Notes, and TeamWare TeamOf-
fice support multimedia data structures in document imaging
features. Other vendors whose products include some multimedia features are AT&T Global Information Solutions, Documentation, Enable Software, Filenet, ForeEnd Group, IBM,
Keyfile, Microsoft, Network Imaging Systems, Pacer Software,
Recognition International, Trax Softworks, Vantage Technologies, ViewStar, Wolf Communications, and Xsoft Division of
Xerox.

Spotlight on the Future

A major trend in work group computing is the development
of better linkages between messaging groupware products and
databases. Another trend is the provision of multiplatform
groupware products to automate business tasks and processes
across DOS, Windows, Macintosh, and UNIX platforms trans-
parently to the user. Most recently, increased use of intranets in
secure corporate environments is also being put to groupware
application use. In the near future, more management tools for
measuring server, linkage, dynamic rerouting, and load-balanc-
ing performance will be included in groupware. As high-speed
LANs and WANs become more common, more multimedia features will be included. In particular, groupware may support
various forms of multiuser multimedia conferencing in realtime. Since groupware has characteristics similar to those of artificial intelligence, it may share the same fate. In the future,
groupware will be everywhere attached or embedded to videoconferencing and database applications but invisible as a distinct product.

12

Racing Along the Information Superhighway

The telecommunications revolution is a result of continual de-regulation and rapid introduction of new, more effective transmission technologies—such as fiber optics and digital wireless—that create low-cost calling, intense competition, and massive restructuring in existing organizations. Today, anyone can start an information transmission business.

Mounting competition exists among local and long-distance telephone companies, cable TV networks, gas and oil pipelines, railroads, power utilities, and even turnpike authorities. All of those entities control information transmission networks or rights of way and are, or can be, parts of the information superhighway infrastructure.

More important, the intensifying competition is leading to universal development of high-speed transmission facilities extended to individual households. Major competitive battles, however, will be fought between services and content delivery to users and subscribers, the arena where interactive multimedia communications is of paramount importance.

What Is the Information Superhighway Anyway?

The **information superhighway** means different things to different people. Theoretically any electronic system of data storage and transmission that can communicate with all the other systems is part of the information superhighway. There are, to be sure, issues of protocol, interfaces, bandwidth, and security that are expected to be solved as time progresses.

Elements of the information superhighway consist of diverse networks that may, or may not, as yet communicate with each other: telephone services, corporate LANs and WANs, the Internet, online services, cable TV, interactive TV, and the extensive communications networks operated by power utilities and the railroads. All of these network infrastructures are capable of transmitting interactive multimedia communications. Not all do it efficiently, and some are restricted by law from providing services to the public. Nevertheless, in the current climate of global deregulation of telecommunications services, all of these network infrastructures must be considered as potential information superhighway tributaries.

The Promise of the Internet

Perhaps more than any other network, the Internet has been synonymous with the information superhighway. Although it is chaotic and unpredictable, it has huge numbers of global users, and many enterprises are looking for ways to exploit it as an interactive multimedia communications infrastructure. The Internet Society estimates 1 million networks and 1 billion users will be on the Internet by the year 2000.

> Caution: The Internet is only one element, and it is not the best infrastructure for transmitting multimedia trafÆc. Many of its links have no capacity to transmit multimedia data and Æles in reasonable time. Another drawback is its inherent insecurity of data transmissions deterring most businesses from offering credit transactions on it.

In corporate environments more interest is now being shown in development of intranets that are based on Internet standards but operate behind secure firewalls on company LANs and WANs.

The World Wide Web

The World Wide Web (WWW), also known as the Web or W3, is the multimedia aspect of the Internet. Developed at CERN, the Swiss particle physics research center in Geneva, it consists of a community of networked resources that deliver multimedia files to users on request. Documents on servers linked to each other are marked up in hypertext transmission protocol mode (HTTP) format. The result is that text, graphics, audio, and video can be accessed on demand.

The use of WWW requires software known as a **browser**. Mosaic, the most popular browser, is a Windows-like interface, and it is credited with changing the complex UNIX command line of the Internet interface into a more user-friendly GUI. Mosaic allows users to browse all kinds of multimedia documents stored in WWW servers. At least, a million copies of the original free Mosaic software have been acquired and WWW is making Internet a mass medium for interactive home shopping, banking, and other uses. More sophisticated commercial browsers have data encryption capabilities, which makes them suitable to perform credit card transactions.

WWW provides access to graphics and video materials based on client-servers that users can navigate using hypermedia documents. Most recently the 3-D WebSpace browser introduced by Silicon Graphics has dramatically changed the experience of cruising the Web. It allows spinning, rotation, and walk-through simulations and is based on virtual reality modeling language (VRML), making the Web even more attractive to conduct electronic commerce.

> Cautionary note: The uneven bandwidth of the Internet infrastructure makes the retrieval of multimedia data often frustrating and unpredictable, although special services are being designed to alleviate the problems.

WWW is projected to have 22 million users by the year 2000, clearly a resource to be considered. It should not, however, be seen as a ready-built alternative for an effective competitive interactive multimedia communications system. It is a component of the information superhighway with multimedia transmission facilities but lacking realtime capabilities. WWW is a resource available to those equipped to access that area of the Internet. It is also being implemented on many corporate intranets in secure networking environments.

Who Uses the Web

Originally set up to serve the scientific and engineering communities in exchanging data, graphics, and images, increasingly the Web is being used by businesses for product and service advertising using images, text, photographs, and video. In January 1993 there were fifty WWW servers identified. The number rose to 7,000 in two years and is estimated to be doubling every two months. Over seventy-seven of the top 1,000 companies in America are represented on the Web, among them American Airlines, AT&T, Ford, GE, IBM, Mobil, and Reebok International.

The first potential market is business-to-business communications, followed by business-to-consumer. Although electronic sales promotion can reach only Internet users, *not* the public at large, the WWW transcends time zones and offers twenty-four-hour interactive multimedia communications. An automobile dealership, for example could use the Web to create a virtual showroom on the Internet, with users getting to see the latest car models. The WWW server could also include the ability to order spare parts and provide access to the manuals that auto repair shops use, allowing users to determine the time involved in an automobile repair job. Grant's Flower and Greenhouses in Ann Arbor, Michigan, had a special display set up in cyberspace by an access provider for $28 per month. Its pages displayed flower arrangements that could be ordered over the Internet. Similarly, PC Flowers of Stamford, Connecticut, established a PC Gifts and Flowers home page on the Web of advertising only, showing products ranging from floral arrangements to stuffed animals. Restaurants and food chains use the Web too. A server displays images of various dishes, and waiters or chefs provide descriptions and commentary by voice, with background music projecting the atmosphere of the establishment.

Exhibit 12-1 shows other potential uses.

Exhibit 12-1. Commerce categories on World Wide Web.

Form of Activity	*Description and Comments*
Promotional	Represented by simple ``cyberbillboards'' with which companies announce their products. A form of electronic institutional advertising
Advertising	Interactive services supported by advertisers Easy navigation from multimedia screens to home pages of advertisers at the discretion of the viewer
Services	Interactive multimedia transmissions offering information about real estate, job locations, travel destinations, one-time events, restaurant guides, etc.
Transactional	Online cybermalls with various electronic storefronts are the best example in this category of interactive commerce
Subscription	Various electronic events during which users are enticed to subscribe. Often some information is made available free, but more desirable data must be paid for

Setting up a Web Server

In the past, Internet servers were expensive systems costing between $15,000 and $50,000. Today, multitasking platforms, with powerful central processors and a lot of RAM, will suffice. RISC-based workstations can handle hundreds of thousands of transactions daily, although the number decreases drastically when handling multimedia video materials. Cost of sales on the Internet averages about twenty cents compared with about the five dollars per mail-order-house sale. Yet despite heavy access and inquiries, very few sales have been recorded by WWW merchants.

For storing multimedia documents and files, the server should be able to accept small-computer system interface (SCSI) disk drives, and for transmission of multimedia traffic, meet the **integrated services digital network**, which provides 128 Kbps of bandwidth. Aside from hardware set-up, it is necessary to prepare the home page representing the vendor on the Web server. This can be done internally or through an outside service with experience in setting up multimedia home pages for WWW servers.

Home pages can be set up for individuals, small businesses, or corporations. All that is needed is the hypertext markup language software, a word processor, and a browser to open and view the created file. Some browsers provide thumbnail-sized images, which save bandwidth and speed up retrieval and can be expanded to full size if needed.

WWW presentations should have the following characteristics.

1. Content that is meaningful, informative, and interesting.
2. Visually compelling message delivery that positions the product in an entertaining way.
3. Interactivity achieved through user involvement in the response mechanism.
4. Presentations that change and provide compelling reasons, and perhaps incentives, for users to return.

Most videos require huge amounts of storage, so transmission takes a very long time over standard telephone lines. For this reason, very small images are used in initial searching, and most of the actual video displays are usually limited to just a few seconds.

Innovative Superhighway Uses

Storefronts and Cybermalls

Merchants can set up electronic storefronts on WWW, providing layers of marketing materials and interactively answering most prospect questions. Users can define their own path of information retrieval, which can include press releases, technical manuals, graphics, animation, voice comments, and video.

The problem: Not all users have PCs or network connectivity adequate to transmit multimedia materials effectively.

Whether business managers and owners choose to design the marketing pages themselves or hire an expert consulting firm, there still remains the matter of setting up the WWW server, which becomes the virtual storefront of the company on the information superhighway. It can be done on the Internet or the commercial online services, but the advantage in doing it on the Web is that users pay only for access, not connect time. As a result, users are likely to spend more time surfing, with a better chance of finding and receiving the promotion.

Online services, nevertheless, are setting up **cybermalls**— shopping mall simulations. Merchants rent a storefront in the cybermall without worrying about the WWW server design. Their only concern is their own home page presentations. Electronic Mall on Compuserve online service, which started in 1985, is the oldest. Its 150 electronic storefronts include JC Penney, Sears Roebuck, Land's End, Brooks Brothers, the Metropolitan Museum of Art, and 800-Flowers.

Announced in 1995 by MCI, MarketplaceMCI is the largest cybermall. MarketplaceMCI is a secure Internet shopping environment combining all the required elements into a specialized service. Fourteen consumer and business companies, including Sara Lee Corporation, have already opened storefronts in the cybermall, and more are following. MarketplaceMCI handles the development and maintenance of the Web servers for each storefront, for which companies pay anywhere from $25,000 to $100,000, depending on the complexity of the installation. Storeowners pay monthly rents ranging from $2,000 to $10,000, as well as transaction fees. MarketplaceMCI features toll-free user access and electronic shopping baskets into which purchases can be accumulated from several stores, as well as multimedia news and other services. The MarketplaceMCI is accessible through MCI home page at http://www.internetMCI.com.

Electronic Business Co-op addresses security in purchasing on the Internet by using encryption-capable Web browsers. They allow purchasers to use credit cards in transactions that go through a Tandem WebServer and are passed on to Check-free network for credit approval. The co-op is an organization set up for this purpose by Checkfree, Spyglass, V-One, and Tandem Computers.

Businesses without capabilities to create storefronts can turn to multimedia developers or the Interactive Merchants Association, set up as clearinghouses for collecting home-shopping content for cybermalls. IMA, a video server vendor organized by Micromall, a subsidiary of Microware Systems, develops operating systems for set-top boxes in collaboration with Digital Equipment Corporation. IMA charges between $60,000 and $100,000 to create a store for a client. It also takes a negotiated percentage of sales. Land's End was among the first retailers to sign on.

Interactive Online Catalogs

Corporations use catalogs to inform customers about products or services. In these cases, the companies are using the Internet to dissiminate information about their products, providing answers faster than traditional help desks or human telephone response.

The catalog shopping industry includes hundreds of companies, large and small. Each, no doubt, would be delighted to have an interactive channel of its own. This $50 billion annual industry must change in order to sell its products and services through interactive channels and compete with the new and specialized home shopping firms that are taking advantage of this new marketing infrastructure.

GE Plastics, a $6 billion subsidiary of General Electric, is among the first developers of an online catalog. This catalog, with 1,500 pages of product information, can be accessed by customers around the world on an around-the-clock basis. Within a month of start-up, it experienced 12,000 hits. GE Plastics believes the catalog gives it a competitive advantage by providing answers in minutes compared to three days using telephone and the fastest mail deliveries.

Some retail companies are developing online versions of their catalog and setting up WWW servers. Among them are Spiegel, Robert Redford Sundance Catalog, and Land's End.

Cyberauctions

An innovative use of the information superhighway is the cyberauction, which Lexus used to sell used cars to its dealers. In this case, the information superhighway links are the satellite TV network and telephones. Dealers, equipped with TV sets that display photographs and descriptions of specific Lexus cars for sale, use digital standard telephone sets to register bids, which instantly appear on the screen. Lexus has completed several cyberauctions of previously rented cars as well as cars picked up on the open market. The cyberauction is operated by NTN Communications, which produces live play-along sports and entertainment for bars and lounges. Toyota is also planning similar cyberauctions through NTN.

AuctionLive!, an interactive service of the Arts and Antiques Network, allows viewers of eight cable TV systems in Connecticut, Maryland, Virginia, and Washington, D.C., to watch a gallery-televised art auction and bid by telephone.

Doing Business on Interactive TV

How It's Done

Interactive TV is based on the assumption that existing home TV sets can be equipped with a set-top control box, a powerful computer that can decompress digital video data for display. The set-top links the user. In the near future, interactive TV could involve about 10 percent of over 93 million TV households in the United States. It is still in the experimental stage.

Subscribers to interactive TV can request a movie, a TV program, or a game or access home shopping without concern for scheduling or time of day. They can also respond to TV broadcasts and commercials in realtime or use the system for interactive services on the information highway.

Because of response capabilities, promoters and advertisers using interactive TV acquire better data regarding clients and potential customers. News organizations can poll hundreds of thousands of viewers in virtual realtime as events unfold without telephone contact. Advertisers make immediate sales of products and services presented in commercials.

Interactive TV systems with digital interaction through fiber-optic cable lines can offer up to 500 channels. These systems provide video transmission signals over high-speed optical fiber links to local switching centers, where they are compressed and received through a decompression box connected to TV sets. The amount of intelligence put into the converter box determines the degree of interactivity.

> More important: What is offered to capture the attention of end-users.

Other interactive TV systems use continuous cellular links and satellite transmissions for two-way interaction or transmit control data via radio and receive viewer response by telephone. Exhibit 12-2 illustrates the principles of these alternatives.

It is not certain whether existing networks and the associated hardware and software can handle thousands of requests for movies, games, broadcasts, or shopping simultaneously. At issue here is delivery of service and the accounting of who consumed what, for how long, at what price, and the preparation of an accurate record and billing statement. Sorting out viewer statistics—who requested what, when, with what frequency, and for how long—is another problem to be addressed. The ultimate question is who is willing to pay how much and for what in order to make interactive TV a profitable enterprise.

Searching for the Most Profitable Uses

A number of pilot programs have been conducted to determine the most profitable interactive TV services. Much of the hype has focused on video on demand, but results suggest that this type of service does not provide sufficient revenues to offset heavy investments for transmissions directly to the home. Home shopping, banking, and other services have increased the appeal of interactive TV services.

Interactive TV services providers on the digital superhighway need to find out what consumers want on TV, which services will be profitable, and what is the most effective method

Exhibit 12-2. Alternative interactive TV systems.

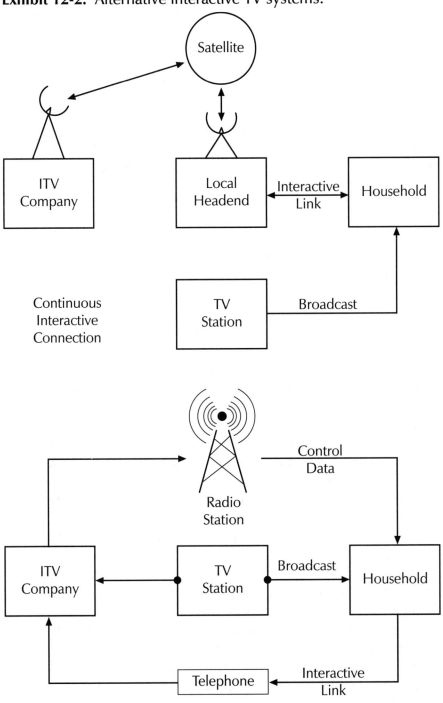

of delivery. To answer these questions, telephone, cable TV, software, and hardware companies have formed partnerships to test consumer acceptance of interactive TV. Exhibit 12-3 outlines the major efforts.

TV tests suggest that the most attractive interactive services are those offering entertainment, related transactional shopping, communications with others, and instant availability of additional information through hypermedia functions. Testing is under way in France, Germany, Italy, Netherlands, Belgium, the United Kingdom, Canada, Australia, Hong Kong, Singapore, and Japan.

Interactive multimedia is now seen as a new means of delivering more entertainment, to more people, more often. It's highly customized for taste, time of engagement, and ability to pay. Business benefits are more precise marketing knowledge and statistics.

Home Shopping

Judging by the success of TV shopping channels that use telephones for order placing, interactive home shopping, which allows immediate response without use of the telephone, has a huge potential. A control unit offers viewers control over products and services viewed so they do not have to waste time looking at products of no interest. Home shopping applications turn the TV set into a merchandising kiosk. The promise of 500 channels offers an opportunity to develop highly targeted promotions based on viewer responses.

Kroger supermarkets experimented first with interactive TV for at-home grocery shopping with same-day delivery. The service is delivered through the Interactive Channel, providing online programming over existing cable TV systems. Subscribers enter their zip code and can then visually roam through the entire store inventory and select items by entering ID numbers. The full grocery order is delivered by Shoppers Express for a $7.95 delivery charge, which can be paid by cash, check, or credit card. After the first shopping experience, a personal delivery list is put together that automatically selects frequently purchased items but remains under the shopper's control.

Exhibit 12-3. Major interactive TV pilot projects.

Service or Pilot	Details of service, sponsors and suppliers
Bell Atlantic	Pilot projects involves 2,000 homes in Alexandria, Arlington, and Fairfax counties in Virginia. Uses Oracle Media Server.
EON, Inc.	Began life as TV Answer based on Hewlett-Packard computers and radio transmission. Provides games, home shopping, and bill-paying services. Pilot operates in Fairfax County, Virginia
Full Service Network (FSN)	Most ambitious interactive TV pilot to date by Time Warner Cable using Silicon Graphics video servers, AT&T switching, and ScientiÆc-Atlanta control units. Service introduced to 4,000 households in Orlando, Florida, area. Offers movies on demand and electronic mall shopping. Videophone and videoconferencing in the future are being planned.
Interactive Network	Backed by NBC, A. C. Neilsen, United Artists, and cablevision. Uses FM radio transmission. System allows viewers to play TV game shows such as *Jeopardy* and *Wheel of Fortune* and to watch select sporting events. Discontinued in 1996.
Main Street	GTE is testing a cable-based interactive TV system designed to acquire data about shopping, travel, games, local information, and referencing services usage patterns.
One Touch	Viacom and AT&T joint venture testing video-on-demand services in Littleton, Colorado, and Castro Valley, California. Initial tests are in 1,000 homes, to be expanded to 4,000.
Prodigy	The IBM/Sears joint venture is adding interactive TV features using Jerrold/General Instrument control units for TV sets.

(continued)

Exhibit 12-3. (continued)

Service or Pilot	Details of service, sponsors and suppliers
U.S. West	Pilot project in 2,500 Omaha, Nebraska, homes planned to expand to 60,000 households. U.S. West has access to FSN technology at Time Warner because it holds 25 percent of that company stock.
Videotron	A Canadian pilot in Montreal, Quebec, tested interactive advertising in four languages during TV broadcasts. Allows selection of video angles and information about players in sports events. Small audiences tested to date.

Home Shopping Network (HSN), a broadcast TV operation, has an interactive presence on the information superhighway. HSN acquired Internet Shopping Network (ISN) and now operates it as a wholly owned subsidiary. Designed to handle 22,000 computer products, ISN sells FTD Flowers, Omaha Steaks, and Hammacher-Schlemmer gifts among its products. It offers 40,000 music titles in twenty-one genres that users can select and download. ISN is based on WWW Netscape Commerce Servers, which provide authentication, data encryption, data integrity, and user authorization, thus ensuring credit security. ISN can be accessed at http://shop.internet.net or at (800) 677-SHOP.

Not all interactive TV pilots have been successful. Time Warner and Spiegel, for example, teamed up to provide the Catalog 1 service on a 24-hour basis seven days a week. The test was eventually reduced to 2 hours once a week. Fingerhut Corporation scrapped a proposed network, and Federated Department Stores shelved the TV Macy's idea after finding out that navigational and purchasing technology is not as simple as it looks.

Online Services Going Multimedia

Online services established some years ago as interactive value-added networks based mostly on text and some graphics are in competition with all the other interactive multimedia services and are developing new multimedia user interfaces (MUI). Some have acquired multimedia marketing and content development ventures to beef up their ability to compete.

Most leading online services are planning or have already established Web servers to provide subscriber access to the Internet online services to advertise and promote their services to users and prospects, making possible advance knowledge of content and where specific materials can be found. On the other hand, online services charge a monthly subscription fee and surcharges for the most desirable materials. Exhibit 12-4 highlights the multimedia capabilities of major online services.

America Online, one of the leading services, acquired Redgate Communications, a multimedia marketing organization. Its objective is to migrate its estimated 5 million users from standard GUI to a multimedia user interface and establish its own Web server presence. Compuserve is also developing a WWW server presence and provides access to Internet for its 2.4 million users, allowing a choice of Web browsers. The company also has a multimedia companion CD-ROM that is updated bimonthly at the user site. It includes video, interviews, movie clips, music, and travelogue materials and provides indirect interactivity. It lacks realtime multimedia capability, however.

Prodigy, one of the oldest consumer-oriented online services, has over 2 million subscribers. It also provides a WWW graphical browser and has its own WWW server. This service permits advertising and as a result is of interest to those who want to promote themselves in cyberspace. Delphi, which established text-based access to WWW a long time ago, is implementing a Netscape Web browser as a main GUI for its online services as well as Internet access. This relatively small service has been acquired by Rupert Murdoch's News Corporation, which promises to change the service into a significant global system.

GEnie, General Electric's online service, is highly technical, with only 350,000 subscribers, but it is famous for having the best multiplayer games. While expensive, this service may become a significant player in the future since video games require extensive multimedia content to stay competitive.

Exhibit 12-4. Multimedia on online services.

Online Service	Major Characteristics and Comments
America Online (800) 848-8199	Estimated 2,000,000 users in mid-1995 Best online publications selection Developed WWW server Multimedia user interface
Compuserve (800) 848-8199	Estimated 2.4 million users Best known for e-mail usage Establishing WWW server Provides choice of WWW browsers Multimedia CD-ROM companion feature
Delphi (800) 776-3449	Implementing Netscape WWW browser as main GUI for online and Internet Early text-based WWW access
GEnie (800) 638-9636	Estimated 350,000 users General Electric technical services Best for multiuser games Relatively expensive
Microsoft Network (206) 882-8080	Latest online service with WWW access interfaces built in Windows 95 Uses Mosaic WWW browser for access to MSN and Internet alike
Prodigy (800) 776-3449	Estimated 2 million users WWW Server launched AstraNet Provides WWW graphical browser Permits advertising Highly consumer oriented

Microsoft's Network (MSN), the latest entrant into online service stakes, takes a new approach in an effort to entice developers and content providers. MSN provides basic services, such as e-mail, and Internet access, but expects to enhance them through partnering with PC vendors, small businesses, news organizations, magazines, family entertainment, reference, and home shopping.

MSN is undercutting traditional fees by charging only

$4.95 a month for basic services. In addition MSN intends to give third-party content and service providers extensive control over pricing and appearance. Competitors claim that bundling of MSN with Windows 95 is unfair unless other online services are given the same opportunity. Through antitrust actions, attempts were made to stop Microsoft. There are over 60 million Windows users, and if only 8 percent of upgraded and new Windows 95 users become MSN subscribers, they will outnumber the 4.7 million online users of all other services combined. Critics nevertheless maintain that content, not infrastructure, is what makes or breaks an interactive network, and this is MSN's biggest challenge.

MSN is expected to provide nodes in over 230 cities. The service supports 14.4 to 128 Kbps and ISDN access facilities. Microsoft is coupling this activity with WWW browsing software from Spyglass, Inc., which is responsible for Mosaic technology. With the Mosaic WWW browser, Microsoft offers users access to MSN and Internet as if both were a single network. This permits users under Windows 95 to acquire, create, and edit WWW documents within Windows applications such as word processors and spreadsheets. In order to increase portability, Microsoft plans to extend MSN client software to Windows NT and Macintosh operating systems. For more details of MSN plans, contact: http://www.microsoft.com or call: (206) 882-8080 or fax: (206) 936-7329.

Some online services are specialized. For example, Philips Media of New York, a subsidiary of the electronic giant Philips NV, developed the Supermarket Trade Network, targeting grocers and packaged goods manufacturers for advertising products to retailers. Another project of the company is a hybrid CD-ROM and online catalog service known as Electronic New Release Book, targeting record retailers. It provides a monthly CD-ROM with music, video, and text covering up to 200 titles and has ordering facilities. The objective of this service providing multimedia elements is, among other things, to reduce the 7 percent error rate in ordering new music products by retailers.

Interactive Gambling

Another service being explored with enthusiasm is interactive gambling. Promoters look to the more than $300 billion wagered annually in gambling enterprises—racetracks, casinos, lotteries, bingo, and other games—and want a piece of the action. It is currently illegal to gamble over interactive TV, but powerful lobbies seek to ease restrictions. Interactive multiuser video games, where prizes take the form of products, services, and instant celebrity status, are seen as a promising new business.

Currently only Connecticut, Kentucky, New York, Ohio, and Pennsylvania permit wagering over the telephone. National interactive gambling requires appropriate legislation in *all* fifty states. Nevertheless, promoters believe that interactive gambling will become a lucrative business, with hundreds of millions of dollars in annual revenues.

NTN Communications, of Carlsbad, California, offers an interactive gaming application called Triples on GTE Main Street. However, money cannot be wagered, and players win prizes ranging from t-shirts to travel packages by betting on live horse races.

Critics maintain that the ease of access will have a corruptive and disruptive influence, and the National Council on Compulsive Gambling is calling for controls, including warnings and wagering limits. Promoters, however, feel that the target audiences for interactive gambling are the same as those for other interactive TV services: middle-aged persons 35 to 55 years of age, with moderate to high incomes, and primarily men (ranging between 65 and 80 percent male). Corporate advertisers are tolerant of gambling in general, and promoters believe they will not be able to bypass such lucrative markets in the interactive TV era.

IWN, in Carlsbad, California, the interactive gaming subsidiary of NTN Communications, is developing a service in which users will download data via TV set-tops and place bets using remote controls. Venues considered include parimutuels, casinos, lotteries, and bingo games.

Bell Atlantic believes that interactive gambling has the potential of becoming the "killer application" of interactive multimedia services and is interested in developing TV-based gambling applications.

ODS Technologies of Tulsa, Oklahoma, is testing interactive wagering on horse races. Bets are placed using remote controls and special TV set-tops with information from the *Daily Racing Form*. ODS expects to charge transaction fees along with advertising revenues.

Hearst Corporation is interested in developing a TV-based gaming service based on a special racing channel. British Airways and Virgin Atlantic plan to introduce in-flight interactive gaming using seat-back terminals for placing bets.

Education

All interactive multimedia service promoters, cable TV, telephone companies, and other interactive TV players have high hopes for multimedia education. This differs from corporate and industrial training designed specifically to provide skills to workers in the virtual corporation and maintain competitiveness in global markets. Consumers may be willing to pay for educational programs. Whether these educational presentations will be used to improve skills and get better jobs, there is still significant potential for interactive multimedia education for cultural and personal interest reasons.

With 500 channels on the information superhighway, many will be dedicated to interactive training, learning, and education in the home. To be competitive and retain attention, educational programs have an element of games. The *Carmen Sandiego* program is often cited as an example. Similar products are available for different age groups. Vocational organizations and correspondence schools are developing educational courseware for networking to subscribers with interactive TV or PCs. Training of contract workers at home can be attractive to virtual corporations because of cost savings and flexibility.

Wireless Multimedia Communications

The ideal solution for portable multimedia communications is digital wireless, also an element on the information superhighway. Its potential must be taken into account by managers in corporations with mobile sales forces or service personnel.

Wireless communications is the ultimate in sales force automation once appropriate service networks are in place.

By the year 2000, about 10 million wireless mobile data network users are expected to exist, according to the Yankee Group, a market research organization specializing in communications.

Motorola, a manufacturer of mobile communications equipment, believes 20 million to 26 million interactive wireless data users will exist by the turn of the century. Other analysts predict the wireless market will skyrocket into a $600 billion a year industry by the year 2010.

Wireless data services solve the problems of portability where plug-in facilities or easy connectivity do not exist—airports and some hotels, for example. Wireless communications provide only local untethered transmission like cellular phones and otherwise rely on proprietary WAN systems to transmit and distribute data on a long-distance basis. Existing wireless services handle voice and data, such as e-mail, but it is clear that video transmissions will be a part of the future.

Videoconferencing With Anybody From Anywhere

Personal digital assistants (PDAs) and personal communications systems (PCSs) are also part of the information superhighway, but these devices have limited multimedia capabilities because of their reliance on wireless communications. Nevertheless, these systems are whetting the appetites of corporate managers for mobile videoconferencing, the ultimate in real-time interactive multimedia communications.

Mobile videoconferencing is in the developmental stage. Video capture and compression boards, developed for powerful notebook computers, can be turned into mobile videoconferencing terminals once a video camera is added. Satellite Learning Corporation of Houston plans to use mobile videoconferencing for teaching vocational skills to welfare recipients. Several hardware manufacturers are developing the appropriate peripherals for use with notebooks. Videoconferencing software is widely available. Toshiba and Intel have joined forces to develop Intel's ProShare videoconferencing and data-sharing application for Toshiba notebooks.

The abillity to transmit and receive images at any location from a specialized corporate server, updated with the latest data and product information, is irresistible and highly competitive. The advent of the first mobile videoconferencing means that business managers should be planning for network transmission facilities and personal communications devices that will give a competitive edge in such an environment.

Mobile videoconferencing will rapidly become universal as an interactive multimedia communications tool, once again leveling the field for everybody in the marketplace. Winners will be those who develop and deliver the most compelling presentation.

Become involved with interactive multimedia communications now, and keep an eye on the future. One thing is certain: Your objective must be to find out what is needed, acquire it, deliver it, and service it faster than your competition. Without interactive multimedia communications and the capability to navigate cyberspace, you'll be way off the highway.

Appendix
Major Multimedia Vendors

This appendix provides an alphabetized list of many of the vendors mentioned throughout the book. Keep in mind that interactive multimedia communications is a new and highly fluid industry, and the company names, addresses, and telephone and fax numbers may change without notice. Additionally, new ventures are being formed rapidly, and there is a lot of merger and acquisition activity among companies in these categories.

Affinity Communications Co.
7 Desoto Road, Essex, MA 01929
Tel: (508) 768-7480
Fax: (508) 768-7474

AimTech Corporation
20 Trafalgar Square, Nashua, NH 03063-1973
Tel: (603) 883-0220, (800) 289-2884
Fax: (603) 883-5582

AITech International
47971 Fremont Boulevard, Fremont, CA 94538
Tel: (510) 226-8960
Fax: (510) 226-8996

Alantec
70 Plumeria Drive, San Jose, CA 95134
Tel: (408) 955-9000

Allen Communications
Wayside Plaza II, 5225 Wiley Post Way, Suite 140,
    Salt Lake City, UT 84116
Tel: (801) 537-7805
Fax: (801) 537-7805

American Mobile Satellite Corp.
1150 Connecticut Avenue, NW, Washington, DC 20036
Tel: (202) 331-5858
Fax: (202) 331-5861

Analog Devices
1 Technology Way, P.O. Box 9106, Norwood, MA 02062
Tel: (617) 329-4700
Fax: (617) 326-8703

Andersen Consulting
69 West Washington Street, Chicago, IL 60602
Tel: (312) 580-0069

Apple Computer, Inc.
20525 Mariani Avenue, Cupertino, CA 95014
Tel: (408) 974-6025

Applix, Inc.
112 Turnpike Road, Westborough, MA 01581
Tel: (800) 827-7549, (508) 870-0300
Fax: (508) 366-9313

Ardis Company
300 Knightsbridge Parkway, Lincolnshire, IL 60069
Tel: (708) 913-1215

Ascom Timeplex Inc.
400 Chestnut Ridge Road, Woodcliff Lake, NJ 07675
Tel: (800) 275-8550, (813) 530-9475, (201) 391-1111

Ask*Me Multimedia Inc.
7100 Northland Circle, Suite 401, Minneapolis, MN 55428
Tel: (612) 531-0603
Fax: (612) 531-0645

AST Research Inc.
16215 Alton Parkway, P.O. Box 57005, Irvine, CA 92619-7005
Tel: (714) 727-4141, (800) 876-4278
Fax: (714) 727-9355

AT&T Global Business Video Services Group
51 Peachtree Center Avenue, Atlanta, GA 30303
Tel: (800) 843-3646, (908) 658-6000

AT&T Microelectronics
555 Union Boulevard, Allentown, PA 18103
Tel: (800) 327-2447, (215) 439-6011
Fax: (215) 778-4106

Avid Technology, Inc.
One Metropolitan Park West, Tewksbury, MA 01876
Tel: (800) 949-AVID
Fax: (508) 851-0418

Banyan Systems Inc.
120 Flanders Road, P.O. Box 5013, Westboro, MA 01581-5013
Tel: (508) 898-1760
Fax: (508) 836-3277

Bell Atlantic
1320 North Courthouse Road, Arlington, VA 22201
Tel: (800) 442-0455

Best Data Products
9304 Deering Avenue, Chatsworth, CA 91311
Tel: (800) 632-2378, (818) 773-9600
Fax: (818) 773-9619

Beyond, Inc.
17 Northeast Executive Parkway, Burlington, MA 01808
Tel: (800) 845-8511, (617) 229-0006

Broadband Technologies
4024 Stirrup Creek Drive,
    Research Triangle Park, NC 27709-3737
Tel: (919) 544-3459
Fax: (919) 544-3459

Broderbund Software, Inc.
500 Redwood Boulevard, P.O. Box 6121, Novato, CA 94948-4560
Tel: (415) 382-4400
Fax: (415) 382-4582

BT North America
2560 North First Street, P.O. Box 49019, San Jose, CA 95161
Tel: (408) 922-0250, (800) 872-7654

Cabletron Systems
35 Industrial Way, Rochester, NH 03867-0505
Tel: (603) 337-2705, (603) 332-9400

CADAM Inc.
1935 North Buena Vista Street, Burbank, CA 91504
Tel: (818) 841-9470

Cardinal Technologies
1827 Freedom Road, Lancaster, PA 17601
Tel: (800) 233-0187, (717) 293-3000
Fax: (717) 293-3055

CBT Systems USA, Ltd.
400 Oyster Point Boulevard, South San Francisco, CA 94080
Tel: (415) 737-9050
Fax: (415) 737-0377

C-Cube Microsystems
399-A West Trimble Road, San Jose, CA 95131
Tel: (408) 944-6300
Fax: (408) 944-6314

Cellular Data Inc.
2860 West Bayshore Road, Palo Alto, CA 94303
Tel: (415) 856-9800
Fax: (415) 856-9888

Centigram Corporation
91 East Tasman Drive, San Jose, CA 95134
Tel: (408) 944-0250
Fax: (408) 942-3562

Chipcom Corporation
Southborough Office Park, 118 Turnpike Road,
    Southborough, MA 01772
Tel: (508) 460-4900

CIMLINC Inc.
1222 Hamilton Parkway, Itasca, IL 60143-1138
Tel: (708) 250-0090
Fax: (708) 250-8513

Cirrus Logic, Inc.
3100 West Warren Avenue, Fremont, CA 94538
Tel: (510) 623-8300

Cisco Systems, Inc.
P.O. Box 3075, 1525 O'Brien Drive, Menlo Park, CA 94025-1451
Tel: (415) 326-1941

Claris Corporation
5201 Patrick Henry Drive, Santa Clara, CA 95052
Tel: (408) 987-7000

Compression Labs, Inc.
2860 Junction Avenue, San Jose, CA 95134
Tel: (408) 435-3000
Fax: (408) 922-4608

Computer Teaching Corporation
1713 South State Street, Champaign, IL 61820
Tel: (217) 352-6363

Comsell Training, Inc.
500 Tech Parkway, Atlanta, GA 30313
Tel: (404) 872-2500

Concurrent Technology Developers
315 Mountain Highway, North Vancouver, BC V7P 3N4, Canada
Tel: (604) 986-6121
Fax: (604) 980-7121

Conexus, Inc.
5252 Balboa Avenue, San Diego, CA 92117
Tel: (619) 268-3380
Fax: (619) 268-3409
Dallas, TX
Tel: (214) 443-2600

Creative Labs, Inc.
1902 McCarthy Boulevard, Milpitas, CA 92035
Tel: (408) 428-6600

Datapoint Corporation
8400 Datapoint Drive, San Antonio, TX 78229
Tel: (210) 699-7000
Fax: (210) 699-7920

Dataware Technologies, Inc.
222 Third Street, Suite 3300, Cambridge, MA 02142
Tel: (617) 621-0820
Fax: (617) 621-0307

Digicom Systems Inc.
188 Topaz Street, Milpitas, CA 95035
Tel: (408) 262-1277

Digital Equipment Corporation
146 Main Street, Maynard, MA 01754-2571
Tel: (800) DIGITAL, (508) 493-5111
Fax: (508) 841-5681

Digital Vision
270 Bridge Street, Dedham, MA 02026
Tel: (617) 329-5400
Fax: (617) 329-6286

Effective Communications Arts, Inc.
221 West 57th Street, 11th Floor, New York, NY 10019
Tel: (212) 333-5656

Electronic Imagery, Inc.
1100 Park Central Boulevard S., Pompano Beach, FL 33064
Tel: (305) 968-7100
Fax: (305) 968-7319

Enterprise Solutions, Ltd.
32603 Bowman Knoll Drive, Westlake Village, CA 91361
Tel: (818) 597-8943

Eon Inc. (formerly TV Answer)
1941 Roland Clarke Place, Reston, VA 22091
Tel: (703) 715-8600

Excalibur Technologies Corporation
9255 Towne Centre Drive, 9th Floor, San Diego, CA 92121
Tel: (619) 625-7900

Extron Electronics (RGB Systems)
13554 Larwin Circle, Santa Fe Springs, CA 90670
Tel: (800) 633-9876, (310) 802-8804
Fax: (310) 802-2741

FileNet Corporation
3565 Harbor Boulevard, Costa Mesa, CA 92626
Tel: (714) 966-3400

Fisher International Systems Corporation
4073 Mercantile Avenue, Naples, FL 33942
Tel: (800) 237-4510, (813) 643-1500

Fore Systems, Inc.
174 Thorn Hill Road, Warrendale, PA 15086-7535
Tel: (412) 772-6600
Fax: (412) 772-6500

Frontier Technologies Corporation
10201 North Port Washington, Mequon, WI 53092
Tel: (414) 241-4555

Fujitsu Industry Networks
1266 East Main Street, Stamford, CT 06902
Tel: (203) 326-2700
Fax: (203) 326-2701

Gain Technology
1870 Embarcadero Road, Palo Alto, CA 94303
Tel: (415) 813-1800

General Magic Inc.
2465 Latham Street, Mountain View, CA 94040
Tel: (415) 965-0400, (415) 965-1830

Global Information Systems Technology, Inc.
Trade Center South, 100 Trade Center Drive,
      Champaign, IL 61820
Tel: (217) 352-1165

GPT Video Systems, Inc.
2975 Northwood Parkway, Norcross, GA 30071
Tel: (404) 263-4781

Grand Junction Networks, Inc.
4781 Bayside Parkway, Fremont, CA 94538
Tel: (510) 252-0726

GTE Corporation
1 Stamford Forum, Stamford, CT 06904
Tel: (203) 965-3533
Fax: (203) 965-2520

Hewlett-Packard
3000 Hanover Street, Palo Alto, CA 94304
Tel: (415) 857-1501, (800) 637-7740

Hitachi Computer Products (America)
3101 Tasman Drive, Santa Clara, CA 95054
Tel: (408) 986-9770

IBM Corporation
4111 Northside Parkway, Atlanta, GA 30327
Tel: (404) 238-2764
Fax: (404) 238-4302

IBM ImagePlus Systems
208 Harbor Drive, Stamford, CT 06904
Tel: (203) 973-5000

IEV International
3595 South 500 West, Salt Lake City, UT 84115
Tel: (800) 438-6161, (801) 466-9093
Fax: (801) 263-9980

Innsoft International, Inc.
250 West First Street, Suite 240, Claremont, CA 91711
Tel: (909) 624-7907

InSoft, Inc.
Executive Park West One, Suite 307, 4718 Old Gettysburg Road,
    Mechanicsburg, PA 17055
Tel: (717) 730-9501
Fax: (717) 730-9504

Integrated Circuit Systems, Inc.
1271 Parkmoor Avenue, San Jose, CA 95126
Tel: (408) 297-1201
Fax: (408) 925-9460

Integrated Information Technology
2445 Mission College Boulevard, Santa Clara, CA 95054
Tel: (800) 832-0770, (408) 727-1885
Fax: (408) 980-0432

Intel Corporation
2200 Mission College Boulevard, Santa Clara, CA 95052-8119
Tel: (408) 765-1558

Kaleida Labs
1945 Charleston Road, Mountain View, CA 94043
Tel: (415) 966-0472
Fax: (415) 966-0400

Kalpana, Inc.
3100 Patrick Henry Drive, Santa Clara, CA 95054
Tel: (408) 088-1600, (408) 749-1600

Kopin Corporation
695 Myles Standish Boulevard, Myles Standish Industrial Park, Taunton, MA
    02780
Tel: (508) 824-9969
Fax: (508) 822-1391

Kurzweil Applied Intelligence, Inc.
411 Waverly Oaks Road, Waltham, MA 02154
Tel: (617) 893-5151
Fax: (617) 893-6525

Larse Corporation
4600 Patrick Henry Drive, Santa Clara, CA 95052
Tel: (408) 988-6600

Lenel Systems International Inc.
19 Tobey Village Office Park, Pittsford, NY 14534
Tel: (716) 248-9720
Fax: (716) 248-9185

Lightstream Corporation
150 Cambridge Park Drive, Cambridge, MA 02140
Tel: (617) 873-6300
Fax: (508) 262-1111

Lotus Development Corporation
55 Cambridge Parkway, Cambridge, MA 02142
Tel: (800) 448-2500, (617) 577-8500

Macromedia, Inc.
600 Townsend Street, San Francisco, CA 94103
Tel: (415) 252-2000
Fax: (415) 626-0554

Matrox
1055 St. Regis Boulevard, Dorval, QB H9P 2T4, Canada
Tel: (514) 685-7230
Fax: (514) 685-7030

MCI Communications Corporation
1801 Pennsylvania Avenue, NW, Washington, DC 20006
Tel: (800) 933-9029, (202) 872-1600
Fax: (202) 887-2443

Media Vision
3185 Laurelview Court, Fremont, CA 94538
Tel: (510) 770-8600, (800) 348-7116
Fax: (510) 770-8648

MediaStar Corporation
14440 Cherry Lane Court, Suite 212, Laurel, MD 20707
Tel: (301) 206-9010

Meridian Data, Inc.
5615 Scotts Valley Drive, Scotts Valley, CA 95066
Tel: (408) 438-3100

MFS Datanet, Inc.
55 South Market Street, Suite 1250, San Jose, CA 95113
Tel: (408) 975-2200

Microsoft Corp.
1 Microsoft Way, Redmont, WA 98052
Tel: (206) 882-8080
Fax: (206) 936-7329

Mitsubishi Electronics America
5665 Plaza Drive, P.O. Box 6007, Cypress, CA 90630
Tel: (714) 220-2500

Motorola Inc.
1303 East Algonquin Road, Schaumburg, IL 60196
Tel: (708) 576-5000

Multimedia Learning, Inc.
5215 North O'Connor, Suite 200, Irving, TX 75039
Tel: (214) 869-8282

nCube, Inc.
919 East Hillsdale Boulevard, Foster City, CA 94404
Tel: (800) 654-2823, (415) 593-9000
Fax: (415) 508-5408

NEC America Inc.
1525 West Walnut Hill Lane, Irving, TX 75038
Tel: (800) 222-4NEC

New Media Graphics
780 Boston Road, Billerca, MA 01821
Tel: (508) 663-0666
Fax: (503) 663-6678

Netedge Systems Inc.
P.O. Box 14993, Research Triangle Park, NC 27709-4993
Tel: (800) 638-3343

New Media Graphics Corporation
780 Boston Road, Billerica, MA 01821
Tel: (508) 663-0666, (800) 288-2207
Fax: (508) 663-6678

Newbridge Networks Corporation
P.O. Box 13600, 600 March Road, Kanata, Ontario,
Canada K2K 2E6
Tel: (613) 591-3600, (800) 343-3600
Fax: (613) 591-3680

Next Computer, Inc.
900 Chesapeake Drive, Redwood City, CA 94063
Tel: (415) 366-0900

Nikon Electronic Imaging
1300 Walt Whitman Drive, Melville, NY 11747
Tel: (516) 547-4200
Fax: (516) 547-0306

Northern Telecom
3 Robert Speck Parkway, Mississauga, Ontario
     L4Z 3C8, Canada
Tel: (416) 897-9000

Novell, Inc.
122 East 1700 South, Provo, UT 84606
Tel: (800) 453-1267

Ntergaid, Inc.
2490 Black Rock Turnpike, Fairfield, CT 06430
Tel: (203) 380-1280, (800) 859-5218

Octel Communications Corporation
890 Tasman Drive, Milpitas, CA 95035
Tel: (408) 942-6500
Fax: (408) 942-6599

Octus Inc.
9940 Barnes Canyon Road, San Diego, CA 92121
Tel: (619) 452-9400
Fax: (619) 452-2427

Opcom/VMX, Inc.
2115 O'Nel Drive, San Jose, CA 95131
Tel: (408) 441-1144
Fax: (408) 441-7026

Optibase, Inc.
7800 Deering Avenue, Canoga Park, CA 91304
Tel: (818) 719-6566, (800) 451-5101
Fax: (818) 712-0126

Optika Imaging Systems Inc.
5755 Mark Dabling Boulevard, Suite 100,
    Colorado Springs 80919
Tel: (719) 548-9800

Optivision, Inc.
1477 Drew Avenue, Suite 102, Davis, CA 95616
Tel: (800) 562-8934, (916) 756-4429
Fax: (916) 756-1309

Oracle Corporation
500 Oracle Parkway, Redwood Shores, CA 94065
Tel: (800) 633-0583, (415) 506-7000
Fax: (415) 506-7200

Panasonic Broadcast & TV Systems
Two Panasonic Way, Secaucus, NJ 07094
Tel: (201) 348-7000
Fax: (201) 392-4482

Performax
3683 Post Road, Southport, CT 06490
Tel: (203) 254-1869

PictureTel Corporation
One Corporation Way, Peabody, MA 01960
Tel: (508) 977-9500
Fax: (508) 977-9481

PowerSoft
70 Blanchard Road, Burlington, MA 01803
Tel: (800) 395-3525, (617) 229-2200
Fax: (617) 272-2540

Projectavision, Inc.
One Penn Plaza, Suite 2122, New York, NY 10119
Tel: (212) 971-3000

ProtoComm Corporation
2 Neshaminy Interplex, Trevose, PA 19053
Tel: (215) 245-2040

Qualcomm, Inc.
6455 Lusk Boulevard, San Diego, CA 92121
Tel: (619) 587-1121
Fax: (619) 658-2110

Racotek Inc. (Raconet)
7401 Metro Boulevard, Suite 500, Minneapolis, MN 55439
Tel: (612) 832-9800

Radius
1710 Fortune Drive, San Jose, CA 95131
Tel: (408) 434-1010
Fax: (408) 954-1927

RAM Mobile Data Inc.
745 Fifth Avenue, Suite 1900, New York, NY 10151
Tel: (212) 373-1930, (212) 303-7800
Fax: (212) 308-5205

Scenario Systems
3 Bridge Street, Newton, MA 02158
Tel: (617) 965-6458

SCO (The Santa Cruz Operation)
400 Encinal Street, Santa Cruz, CA 95061
Tel: (408) 425-7222

ShareVision Technology, Inc.
1901 McCarthy Boulevard, Milpitas, CA 95035
Tel: (408) 428-0330
Fax: (408) 428-2389

Sierra Network
41486 Old Barn Way, Oakhurst, CA 93644
Tel: (209) 642-0700
Fax: (209) 642-0888

Sierra On-Line, Inc.
40033 Sierra Way, Oakhurst, CA 93644
Tel: (209) 683-4468
Fax: (209) 683-3633

Sigma Designs
46501 Landing Parkway, Fremont, CA 94538
Tel: (510) 770-0100
Fax: (510) 770-2640

Silicon Graphics, Inc.
2011 North Shoreline Boulevard, Mountain View,
    CA 94043-1389
Tel: (800) 800-4SGI, (415) 960-1980
Fax: (415) 961-0595

Spectrum
9 Oak Park Drive, Bedford, MA 01730
Tel: (800) 227-1127, (617) 271-0500
Fax: (617) 275-5644

Spectrum Microsystems, Inc.
320 Storke Road, Goleta, CA 93117
Tel: (805) 968-5100

Spectrum Signal Processing
1500 West Park Drive, Westborough, MA 01581
Tel: (800) 323-1842, (508) 366-7355
Fax: (508) 898-2772

SP Telecom
60 Spear Street, San Francisco, CA 94105
Tel: (800) 229-7782, (415) 905-4000

Sprint Video
71 West 95th, Overland Park, MO 66212
Tel: (800) 669-1235, (913) 624-3000
Fax: (913) 624-3281

Starlight Networks, Inc.
325 East Middlefield Road, Mountain View, CA 94043
Tel: (415) 967-2774

Storm Technology, Inc.
1861 Landings Drive, Mountain View, CA 94043
Tel: (415) 691-6620, (415) 691-9825

StrataCom Inc.
1400 Parkmoor Avenue, San Jose, CA 95126
Tel: (408) 294-7600

Structural Dynamics Research Corporation, Inc.
2000 Eastman Drive, Milford, OH 45150-2789
Tel: (513) 576-2096
Fax: (513) 576-2135

SunSoft, Inc.
2550 Garcia Avenue, Mountain View, CA 94043
Tel: (415) 960-3200

SuperMac Technology
485 Portero Avenue, Sunnyvale, CA 94086
Tel: (800) 345-9777, (408) 245-2202
Fax: (408) 735-7250

Sybase Corporation
6475 Christie Avenue, Emeryville, CA 94608
Tel: (510) 596-3500

Synernetics, Inc.
85 Rangeway Road, North Billerica, MA 01862
Tel: (508) 670-9009

Synesis Corporation
200 Hembree Circle Drive, Roswell, GA 30076
Tel: (404) 475-6788
Fax: (404) 442-0674

SynOptics Communications
4401 Great American Parkway, Santa Clara, CA 95054
Tel: (408) 988-2400
Fax: (408) 988-5525

Technology Applications Group, Inc.
1700 West Big Beaver Road, Troy, MI 48084
Tel: (313) 649-5200

Telco Systems, Inc., Network Access Division
4305 Cushing Parkway, Fremont, CA 94538
Tel: (800) 776-8832, (510) 490-3111
Fax: (510) 656-3031

3DO Company
600 Galveston Drive, Redwood City, CA 94063
Tel: (415) 261-3000
Fax: (415) 261-3120

Time Warner Inc.
1271 Avenue of the Americas, New York, NY 10020
Tel: (212) 522-1626

United Medical Network Corporation
708 South Third Street, Suite 400, Minneapolis, MN 55415
Tel: (800) 991-4866, (612) 330-0990
Fax: (612) 330-0989

Verimation, Inc.
50 Tice Boulevard, Woodcliff Lake, NJ 07675
Tel: (800) 967-6366

Viacom International, Inc.
1515 Broadway, New York, NY 10036-5794
Tel: (212) 258-6508
Fax: (212) 258-6497

Videoconferencing Systems Inc.
5801 Goshen Springs Road, Norcross, GA 30071
Tel: (404) 242-7566

VideoLabs, Inc.
5270 West 84th Street, Minneapolis, MN 55437
Tel: (612) 897-1995
Fax: (612) 897-3597

VideoLogic Inc.
245 First Street, Cambridge, MA 02142
Tel: (617) 494-0530

Videoserver, Inc.
5 Forbes Road, Lexington, MA 02173

Tel: (617) 863-2300

Videotex Systems, Inc.
8499 Greenville Avenue, Dallas, TX 75081
Tel: (214) 234-1769, (800) 326-3576
Fax: (214) 994-6475

VTEL Corporation (formerly Video Telecom)
1901 West Braker Lane, Austin, TX 78758
Tel: (800) 284-8871, (512) 834-9734
Fax: (512) 834-3794

Wang Laboratories Inc.
One Industrial Avenue, Lowell, MA 01851
Tel: (508) 459-5000

Weingarten Publications
38 Chauncey Street, Boston, MA 02111
Tel: (617) 542-0146

Wellfleet Communications, Inc.
8 Federal Street, Billerica, MA 01821
Tel: (508) 670-8888
Fax: (508) 436-3658

Westbrook Technologies Inc.
22 Pequot Park Road, P.O. Box 910, Westbrook, CT 06498
Tel: (800) WHY-FILE

Wicat
1875 South State Street, Orem, UT 84058
Tel: (801) 224-6400

WordPerfect Corporation
1555 North Technology Way, Orem, UT 84057-2399
Tel: (800) 451-5151, (801) 225-5000
Fax: (801) 222-5077

Workstation Technologies, Inc.
18010 Skypark Circle, Irvine, CA 92714
Tel: (714) 250-8983
Fax: (714) 250-8969

Xing Technology Corporation
1540 West Branch Street, Arroyo Grande, CA 93420
Tel: (800) 295-6458, (805) 473-0145
Fax: (805) 473-0147

Xyplex Inc.
330 Codman Hill Road, Boxborough, MA 01719
Tel: (800) 338-5316, (508) 246-9900
Fax: (508) 264-9930

Glossary

A/D—analog-to-digital conversion Usually refers to an A/D converter device that basically digitizes a continuous waveform analog signal into a digital bit stream. It includes the steps of sampling and quantizing.

ADSL—asymmetrical digital subscriber line A consumer telephone line whose bandwidth has been enhanced to higher-capacity levels. It can provide video-on-demand services over a distance of up to 18,000 feet of existing copper wire.

algorithm A sequence of processing steps that performs a particular operation, such as compressing a digital image.

aliasing Undesirable visual effects in video, usually caused by inadequate sampling. Jagged edges or curved object boundaries are the most common problems. *Antialiasing* refers to software that adjusts such effects. *See also* artifact.

animation Movement of an object on a screen from point to point (path) or displayed sequentially at specific time intervals (cycle).

ANSI—American National Standards Institute A membership organization, existing since 1918, that coordinates the development of standards in private and public sectors. It deals, among others, with standards pertaining to programming languages, telecommunications, and storage media. ANSI represents the United States at the International Standards Organization (ISO).

API—application program interface Formats of messages used to activate and interact with functions of another program.

APPN—advanced peer-to-peer networking A distributed client-server networking feature that IBM added to its Systems Network Architecture (SNA) designed to support efficient and transparent sharing of applications in a distributed computing environment.

artifact An unnatural or unintended object observed in the reproduction of an image in a video system.

ASIC—application-specific integrated circuit A semicustom chip used in a specific application that is designed by combining certain existing integrated circuit patterns known as standard cells from a library maintained by semiconductor manufacturers. Such designs are faster and sometimes cheaper than designing a new microchip from scratch.

aspect ratio   The ratio between the number of horizontal and vertical pixels (the smallest elements or picture elements) on a display screen. Determines the possible width and height of images at a particular resolution.

asymmetric system   A video storage and display system that requires more devices and processing to compress and store than to play back an image.

asynchronous   A method of transmission that does not require a common clock but separates fields of data by stop-and-start bits.

ATM—asynchronous transfer mode   A high-speed switching platform that can transmit voice, data, and video signals faster and more efficiently than traditional methods. It uses packets of fixed length of 53 bytes and is also known as BISDN or cell relay.

audio   Sound portion of a video signal, or separate sound used to annotate objects on frames such as text, graphics, animation, and still images.

audio buffer   Computer memory segment or separate device for storage of audio data for playback associated with an individual frame.

authoring language   High-level programming language using natural English statements (sometimes known as *mnemonics*) that reflect closely the functions that these commands perform. Such languages are specifically designed for developing multimedia applications, but they also exist in other domains.

authoring system   A software product designed for users without programming skills for developing and testing multimedia applications. Typical examples of the most popular authoring languages are Director, Authorware, Multimedia Toolbook, Quest, and IconAuthor. There are several dozen authoring systems on the market varying in price from $50 to $5,000. The most useful are the high-end products that integrate the many design functions necessary to develop a multimedia application.

bandwidth   The range of frequencies that a given system is able to reproduce; the communications capacity of a transmission line or a specific path through a network measured in bits per second (bps). In a local area network, bandwidth is analogous to throughput.

baseband   A network where the bandwidth is taken up by a single digital signal, such as in Ethernet and token-ring local area networks.

baud   A unit of speed defining the rate of transmission of binary data approximately equal to 1 bit per second (bps) at lower speeds. Common rates of 300, 1,200, 2,400, and 9,600 bps are available from common carriers.

BISDN—Broadband Integrated Services Digital Network. *See* ATM.

bitmap   A sector of memory or storage that contains the pixels that represent an image arranged in the sequence in which they are scanned.

bitmapped graphic   A graphic image that can be accessed on a bit-by-bit (pixel) basis and is directly addressable on the screen.

BLOB—binary large object   An abbreviation applied to describe very large data files such as are representative of multimedia content, which includes audio and video materials. BLOBs can consist of many megabytes of data, each representing an image or a video clip in digital form.

bridge A hardware device with an interface for connecting or extending local area networks (LANs) of the same type or connecting LANs and wide area networks (WANs) regardless of the specific rules (protocols) governing transmission of data. Bridges can be transparent, translating, or encapsulating types.

broadband A network in which multiple signals can share the same bandwidth simultaneously through the use of multiplexing, or splitting, the signal.

browser A user interface for interacting with the World Wide Web servers on the Internet.

CAI—computer-assisted instruction *See* CBT.

CBT—computer-based training

CCITT—Consultative Committee International Telephone and Telegraph An international body that develops standards for voice and video transmission and compression over common carrier and digital networks. It has been renamed the International Telecommunications Union (ITU).

CDDI—copper distributed data interface A version of the fiber distributed data interface (FDDI) standard providing 100 megabits per second bandwidth capacity but implemented on copper wires; consequently, it is more limited in range.

CD-I—compact disk–interactive A multimedia delivery standard introduced by Philips and Sony targeted at consumer and education markets.

CD-ROM—compact disk–read only memory An optical disk storage device standardized for data with 680 megabyte capacity. It can hold about 250,000 pages of text and is used extensively for storing multimedia titles. CD-ROM disks require special CD-ROM drives to play. Multimedia-enabled PCs include a CD-ROM drive as a basic multimedia storage and playback device.

cell relay *See* ATM.

chroma-keying Video terminology dealing with a methodology to replace selected colors on a video image by inserting other colors that allow the creation of different scenes against the background. Also known as *color key*. *See also* chrominance.

chrominance Signals of an image that represent color components such as hue and saturation. A black-and-white image has a chrominance value of zero. Also known as *chroma*.

circuit switching A switching method in which a dedicated path is set up between the transmitter and receiver. The connection is transparent because switches do not attempt to interpret the data.

client-server An architecture and software programs that distribute computing responsibility between a requesting computer (front end), such as a PC or workstation, and a server, or supplying computer (back end)—normally a local area network file server, a minicomputer, or a mainframe. With two or more machines, client-server systems can dramatically reduce network traffic and increase performance.

CMIP—Common Management Information Protocol   A set of telecommunication rules (protocol) developed by IBM and 3Com and endorsed by the International Standards Organization that provides a specification and formats for collecting network management data. An alternative to Simple Network Management Protocol (SNMP), which originated with UNIX operating system and spread to other operating environments.

codec—coder/decoder   A special processor that can digitize analog audio and video signals and decode digital data back into analog form.

compound document   A digital document composed of a variety of data types and formats, each derived from the application that created it—for example, a personnel file in a computer that includes text and photographs of employees, all combined in a single digital file stored in a database.

compression   The translation of video, audio, or digital data singly or in combination to a more compact form for storage and transmission. Computer algorithms and other techniques are used to accomplish this compression process. *See also* JPEG; MPEG.

concurrence   Simultaneous transmission of or occurrence of two or more events or activities within the same time period. In engineering, conceptual design, stress analysis, prototype building, testing, and financing may be taking place at the same time. Each activity generates its own data, which are used throughout the project. Concurrent engineering is a discipline supported by computer programs that allows immediate exchange of such data and improves the performance of all those functions simultaneously, saving time and cost of changes and adjustments at a later stage.

control track   Component of a video signal, exclusive of picture and sound, which provides essential synchronizing information.

conversation   Interaction between user and systems or other users in conferencing networks.

cybermall   Electronic service providing online storefront simulations to interactive users.

cyberspace   Refers to a computer-generated electronic environment that is designed to give the user an artificial feeling of movement and discovery; an interactive system in which a user originates queries or provides inputs, which change the contents and create a specific response. The word was coined by fiction writer William Gibson in the novel *Neuromancer*. The Internet or a corporate local area network is cyberspace because it transmits digital data and changes all the time. Virtual reality is an example of three-dimensional cyberspace in which users can immerse themselves electronically using suitable electronic equipment such as head-mounted displays and gloves.

data rate The speed of data transfer process, normally expressed in bits per second (bps) or bytes per second (Bps).

DCT—discrete cosine transform A complex mathematical algorithm used in compression devices for eliminating redundant data in blocks of pixels on a screen. It is the basis for several compression standards used in multimedia data processing.

digital sampling Recording digital signals representative of a level of sound.

digitizing The process of coverting analog electronic signals into digital format, which can be stored, manipulated, and displayed by a computer. It is accomplished by special A/D converters in the form of audio capture boards, video frame grabbers, scanners, or combinations of those in a single circuit board.

dissolve Gradual fading out of an image on the screen as another appears.

downlink Earth station used to receive signals from satellites.

DSP—digital signal processor A specialized microchip designed to process digitized waveform data of sound and video efficiently. DSPs combine the high speed of a microcontroller with the numerical capabilities of an array processor, which is a computer capable of performing simultaneous computations on elements of an array of data in several dimensions.

DVI —digital video interactive A compression format for recording digital video on a CD-ROM disk that provides up to 72 minutes of full-motion video, 4 hours of one-quarter screen full-motion video, or 14 hours of one-eighth screen full-motion video.

encoding The function of assigning a code or cipher to represent data. In information processing, all data—whether text, graphics, or video—must be encoded into some form of binary code that can be processed by the computer.

enterprise multimedia Multimedia communications capability throughout the corporate environment.

Ethernet A commonly used local area network protocol standard that allows networked PCs or terminals to communicate and transmit packets at any time over coaxial, twisted pair, and fiber optic cabling with up to 10 megabits per second bandwidth capacity. Packet collisions resulting from such transmission freedom can delay a packet during transmission.

fade A gradual change in brightness of an image or intensity or sound; considered to be a special effect.

FDDI—Fiber-Distributed Data Interface A standard developed by ANSI.

FDDI-Sync A variant of FDDI that provides priority to synchronous traffic on the local area network.

FDDI II A special new standard for transmission of signals on local area networks at a specified rate (isochronous); it carries traffic in channels instead of packets as FDDI does.

firewall A security system controlling access to corporate networks.

flicker A phenomenon in a videodisk freeze frame when both video fields are not matched properly; a visible fluctuation brightness of an image.

fps frames per second. *See also* frame rate.

fractal—fractional dimensional Mathematical definition of a fractional element of an image after repeated application of a specific compression algorithm with a theoretical compression ratio capability of 10,000 to 1.

frame A complete image in film or video consisting of two interlaced fields of 525 scan lines running at 30 frames per second (fps), defined by the National TV Standards Committee (NTSC) system used in North America.

frame grabber A digitizer that converts video images into digital data that can be manipulated by a computer program.

frame rate Speed at which frames are displayed on the monitor. Standard broadcast TV rate is 30 frames per second (fps) in North America and 25 fps in Europe. The minimum acceptable movement frame rate is 15 fps.

FSIG—FDDI Synchronous Implementers Group Formed in December 1992 to expedite delivery of standardized distributed multimedia solutions to users.

full-motion video Display of video at the broadcast frame rate of 30 frames per second.

gateway Interfaces designed to convert protocols between two different types of networks.

Gbps Gigabits per second.

genlock Synchronization generator lock. Permits the combination of two or more video sources by synchronizing their signals together to produce a recordable composite video that can contain elements from each source.

GUI—graphical user interface A screen interface with icons that allows direct manipulation of on-screen objects, menus, and dialog controls.

HDTV—high-definition television A TV screen with resolution comparable to a movie theater or 35-mm slide, which requires at least 2 million pixels per frame. Standard TV resolution contains only 336,000 pixels.

headend Facility in a cable system from which all signals originate. It picks up local and distant TV stations and satellite programming and amplifies for retransmission through the system.

home page Initial screen of a World Wide Web site.

hypermedia Defines hypertext, which contains a large percentage of multimedia content, such as graphics, images, audio, and video. *See also* hypertext.

hypertext Linked pieces of text joined together in a nonsequential manner and accessible by navigation through a series of menus.

H.261 An international compression standard of the International Telecommunications Union designed to facilitate the transmission of video images over digital networks at data rates ranging from 64 kilobytes per second to 2.048 megabytes per second and also based on DCT algorithm. Also known as *px64 Kbps standard,* where p = 1,2,3, . . ., 30 and intended primarily for videoconferencing and videotelephony.

IMA—Interactive Multimedia Association An umbrella organization of over 230 suppliers and end users to deal with multimedia standards and data exchange issues.

inferencing engine Logical program of an expert system making artificial intelligence decisions.

intelligent hub A hardware device that provides linkage between various local area networks and automatically accounts for new patterns of interconnections (topology) as changes and expansion take place.

interactivity Action and reaction between end user and computer systems.

interactivity levels Pertains to interactive design features available with respective hardware configurations: Level One, consumer devices; Level Two, industrial devices; Level Three, Levels One and Two interfaced with an external computer and peripherals such as printers, scanners, video cameras, speakers, and microphones. These levels do not relate to quality, values, or sophistication of contents and displays.

interframe coding A video compression technique that concentrates on coding high-detail areas of a picture.

Internet A network of networks linked through a common set of communications rules (protocol) that allows any number of computer networks to link up and act as one.

intraframe coding A video compression technique in which half the picture information is eliminated by discarding every other frame and displaying each frame for twice the normal duration during playback.

ISDN—Integrated Services Digital Network A set of digital network interface standards consisting of a signalling channel and a number of 64 kilobytes per second digital transmission channels that are used to provide circuit switched connections.

ISO—International Standards Organization

isochronous A communications capability that delivers a signal at a specified, defined rate that is desirable for continuous data, such as voice and full-motion video transmitted at 30 frames per second.

ITU—International Telecommunications Union The standards-setting body under the control of United Nations since 1947, which through its committees is responsible for many telecommunications standards pertaining to videoconferencing and audio and video transmissions between equipment from various manufacturers.

ITV—interactive television

JPEG—Joint Photographic Experts Group A standard for compression algorithms for digitizing still images based on DCT with compression ratios ranging from 10-to-1 to 80-to-1.

just-in-time A concept of software instructions available at the point of time when it is needed to explain a procedure.

Kbps—kilobits per second

LAN—local area network A digital communications network capable of transmitting data at high rates between PCs, workstations, servers, and printers in a confined location, such as an office floor or a building. These units are linked with a high-capacity communications link, and transmission is controlled through a special network operating system.

latency   The state of being present but not visible or active; applies to a power or quality that has not yet come into sight or action but may at any time. Used to describe the delay in network transmission of data.

legacy system   Mainframe and minicomputer-based information systems that are critical to Fortune 1000 corporations in running day-to-day operations. About 50 to 80 percent of management information systems budgets are spent on maintenance of those systems.

lossy   A compression technique in which a displayed and decompressed image does not contain all the original digitized data.

lossless   Any compression scheme that allows full recovery of original data.

luminance   Brightness values of all points in an image.

MAN—metropolitan area network   The name sometimes given to high-bandwidth networking facilities in a densely populated region such as a metropolitan area and its suburban business and institutional communities.

mastering   A realtime process in which videotaped materials are used to create a master optical disk, which can be replicated into CD-ROMs.

Mbps—megabits per second.

MCI—media control interface   Platform-independent multimedia specification initiated by Microsoft in 1990 that provides a consistent way to control CD-ROM and video devices.

MCU—multipoint control unit   A device for bridging three or more videoconferencing users of the same or differing protocols.

MHEG—Multimedia and Hypermedia Experts Group   An International Standards Organization activity concerned with coordinating specifications of multimedia design on any platform.

MIDI—Musical Instrument Digital Interface   A series of digital bus standards for interfacing of digital musical instruments with computers.

MIPS—million operations per second

MPC—multimedia PC   Minimum multimedia hardware delivery platform, standard MPC-1 and MPC-2.

MPEG—Motion Picture Experts Group   A standard for digital video compression that records only changes from frame to frame and is based on the DCT algorithm. Compression ratio is a trade-off between motion video quality, size of window, and frame rate.

multimedia   Integration of several media such as text, voice, images, or graphics into a single presentation.

needs analysis   A critical phase of the interactive multimedia design process based on the needs of the end user.

node   Network computer or control point.

NTSC—National Television Standards Committee   Defines North American color TV signal standards in 30 frames per second.

ODB—object data base A database that can handle diverse and complex data, including video, audio, bitmaps, graphics, animation, and unstructured text.

online Hardware devices and services that are in active communication with a central source or system. The three best-known online services are America Online, CompuServe, and Prodigy.

packet switching Transfer of data by means of addressed packets or blocks of information. This differs from circuit switching because the network interprets some data and determines the routing during the transfer of a packet.

PAL Color TV signal format in Europe and some other countries. Uses an interlaced scheme with 25 frames per second and 625 lines per screen.

pixel—picture element The smallest element of a screen represented as a point of specific color and intensity level.

platform Determines a specific hardware architecture and standard for a particular computer model series that is the basis for development of all software for such equipment. Sometimes *platform* refers to a combination of any hardware with a specific operating system, such as DOS, Windows, or UNIX.

primitive A basic element for display, such as a point, arc, line, circle, alphanumeric character, or marker.

px64 *See* H.261.

quantizing The process of converting analog values into digital with a limited number of bits.

RAM—random access memory The basic working memory of a computer in the form of microchips that form part of the central processing unit. Each byte of a RAM device can be accessed directly without regard to bytes before or after it. That is why it is called random access memory.

realtime The transfer of data that returns results so rapidly in actual time that the process appears to be instantaneous to the user.

resolution A measure of image quality of a display. It refers to the number of pixels available on the display and controls the level of detail that can be presented.

RDBMS Relational Data Base Management System.

RGB—red green blue A color display signal consisting of separately controlled red, green, and blue beams, which results in high-quality color output normally used in computer screens.

RIFF—Resource Interchange File Format Platform-independent multimedia specification developed by Microsoft in 1990 that allows audio, image, animation, and other multimedia elements to be stored in a common format.

RISC—reduced instruction set computer Hardware architecture with reduced number of instructions that operates faster than conventional processors.

rollabout system A mobile video conferencing system.

run-length coding A data compression technique that records repeated data elements with the same value only once, along with a count of the number of times they occur.

sampling The process of reading and recording value levels of an analog signal at evenly spaced time intervals. It is a step in the process of digitization prior to encoding.

sampling rate The rate at which sampling occurs during digitization. Audio digitizing may involve sampling of 16 bits of data at rates as high as 48,000 times per second.

SECAM—Sequential Couleur Avec Moniteur The standard for color TV developed in France and also used in Russia, Eastern Europe, and some other countries. It compares with PAL at 25 frames per second, and the interlaced image is made up of 625 lines per frame.

segmentation Topology of a LAN to facilitate multimedia transmission.

smart agent A software routine capable of responding intelligently to questions or actions of a human person.

SMPTE—Society of Motion Pictures and Television Engineers Establishes standards and documentation used in TV production. The SMPTE time code is standard eight-digit code used in identification of frames in the form of HH:MM:SS:FF (hours, minutes, seconds, frame numbers) on audiotape and videotape for synchronization purposes.

SNA—Systems Network Architecture An IBM network strategy that defines communications methods for many IBM systems ranging from PCs to mainframes. Introduced in 1974, it is supported by many vendors.

SNMP—Simple Network Management Protocol A popular protocol that provides specifications and formats for collecting network management data as an alternative to CMIP.

SONET—Synchronous Optical Network A new standard for transmitting a variety of light signals over optical fiber, allowing different fiber systems to interconnect efficiently with an unprecedented level of accuracy and customer control. It includes a hierarchy of transmission rates ranging from 51.5 megabits per second up to 2.4 gigabits per second.

special effects Video image manipulation techniques for enhancing the transition from one image to another or for creating an unusual appearance. Includes effects such as dissolve, fade, and wipe, which are usually included as features in some video boards and authoring systems.

storyboard Basic documentation of the proposed contents of a multimedia application, an advertising spot, or film; prepared screen by screen and includes information about types of video, audio, and other objects that will be used. May also include details of navigational objects and interactivity levels at each point of the application.

synchronous traffic Transmission that requires that a clock signal be transmitted with the data so that both transmitter and receiver can agree on the time-related location of the bits. *Compare to* asynchronous.

TCP/IP—Transmission Control Protocol/Internet Protocol A protocol developed by the Department of Defense to connect dissimilar systems on a network commonly used in UNIX networks.

timeout In an interactive system, the time limit within which a response must occur before a default branch of the program is executed automatically.

time sensitive traffic Real-time data transmission.

token ring A local area network protocol standard requiring network nodes to receive the circulating token—the permission to transmit—before the node can transmit a packet. It is commonly found in IBM's SNA environments.

touch screen Pressure-sensitive display monitor that is often used as a multimedia control instead of or in conjunction with a keyboard. The most sophisticated touch screens also include z-axis control, which allows screen response at different rates depending on the level of pressure applied.

TSS—Telecommunications Standardization Sector Previously known as CCITT.

tweening An animation technique where movement between key frames of a multimedia application is generated by the computer.

ULSI—ultra large-scale integration Generally applies to memory microchips with over 1 megabyte storage capacity and comparable levels of integration for microprocessors and other circuits.

uplink Earth station used for transmitting to satellites.

VCR—video cassette recorder Can be used with appropriate conversion device as input or output for multimedia applications.

videoconferencing Use of voice, with image or video, in communications with remote party over existing networks or public telephone links.

video-dial-tone New public services being introduced for transmitting video signals just like audio telephony.

videodisk An optical disk on which video signals have been recorded most often in NTSC analog format. Widely used as video input source for multimedia training applications.

Video for Windows Microsoft standard that allows end users to view video within a window of their screen.

video-on-demand Interactive TV concept for retrieval of video programs or movies from an interactive service at the consumer's convenience outside of conventional schedules.

video server Special server dedicated to storing and delivering video content.

videotelephony Sending video signals via telephone lines.

videotext Two-way interactive service using either cable or telephone links to connect a central computer to TV screens.

virtual Existing or resulting in an effect although without factual basis. A *virtual memory* is a technique that simulates more memory than is available and allows the running of several programs simultaneously. A *virtual monitor* is a computer that has the ability to reconfigure itself to use different monitors or display the same screen on several monitors simultaneously. A *virtual network* is one that allows users to communicate locally and remotely across all types of networks through a common user interface.

virtual reality The use of computers to simulate real environments with which a user can interact. Also known as artificial reality, cyberspace, and telepresence.

VTR—videotape recorder.

VUI—video user interface A next-generation computing interface metaphor that will use a full-motion video window as part of the user interface and may employ icons to facilitate navigation.

WAN—wide area network A network connecting technologically incompatible devices or local area networks over long distances, typically using common carrier transmission facilities.

whiteboard A feature of multimedia conferencing that allows users at various locations using pointing devices simultaneously to edit, draw on, and annotate documents that include word processing, spreadsheets, graphics, engineering drawings, and video.

Windows 95 The latest PC operating environment with built-in communications and multimedia capabilities developed by Microsoft as an upgrade of the existing Windows versions. It includes special interfaces for connecting PCs to the Microsoft Network and to the Internet.

wipe A special effect in which one image pushes aside another off the screen. Many different approaches exist.

WWW—World Wide Web The multimedia networks of the Internet.

WYSIWYG—What You See Is What You Get A user interface of many authoring systems where the author sees the screens as he or she develops them exactly the way they will appear to the user.

Index